SELF-CARE *for* BLACK WOMEN

SELF-CARE *for* BLACK WOMEN

150 Ways to Radically Accept & Prioritize Your
Mind, Body, & Soul

OLUDARA ADEEYO

ADAMS MEDIA
NEW YORK LONDON TORONTO SYDNEY NEW DELHI

Adams Media
An Imprint of Simon & Schuster, Inc.
100 Technology Center Drive
Stoughton, Massachusetts 02072

First Adams Media hardcover edition January 2022

ADAMS MEDIA and colophon are trademarks of Simon & Schuster.

For information about special discounts for bulk purchases, please contact Simon & Schuster Special Sales at 1-866-506-1949 or business@simonandschuster.com.

The Simon & Schuster Speakers Bureau can bring authors to your live event. For more information or to book an event contact the Simon & Schuster Speakers Bureau at 1-866-248-3049 or visit our website at www.simonspeakers.com.

Interior design by Michelle Kelly
Illustrations by Tess Armstrong

Manufactured in China

10 9 8 7

Library of Congress Cataloging-in-Publication Data has been applied for.

ISBN 978-1-5072-1731-3
ISBN 978-1-5072-1732-0 (ebook)

Dedication

For my mother, who did not live long enough to experience the peace of radical self-care, and all the Black women who are dedicated to choosing their well-being above everything.

Contents

Introduction • 10

Why Black Women Must Practice Self-Care • 12

Part 1: MIND • 21

Part 2: BODY · 77

Part 3: SOUL · 131

Introduction

*H*ey, sis. You stressed? Girl, I know you are. You're a Black woman in a society that constantly oppresses Black people and women. You're at the intersection of these two beautiful identities, but you're forced to navigate a world that throws misogynoir in your face. That is, misogyny directed at Black women, where racism and sexism are at the crux of the mistreatment. *sucks teeth* I'm tired just thinking about it.

So, ask yourself: *When was the last time I practiced some self-care?* I'm talking about taking some time to do something that calms your mind, nourishes your body, and replenishes your soul. An activity or habit that helps you operate as the best version of yourself. I know. You're thinking, *Ain't nobody got time for that.*

But, sis, the real tea is, you can't afford to not make time for that. In a world that tells you that you and your needs do not matter, where Black women are expected to suffer in silence, and where Black women are disproportionately dying at a higher rate from things like heart disease and maternal-related illnesses, self-care is more essential than ever. It is both a form of resistance against these systems of inequality and your self-preservation. This is how you can actively fight back against a societal ecosystem that is hell-bent on beating you down.

Here, you'll find 150 self-care activities specifically designed for Black women by a Black woman (*hey, girl!*) to cultivate and renew your sense of mental, physical, and spiritual wellness, such as:

- Activate a connection to your family's history.
- Create boundaries at work.
- Release feelings of guilt around self-love.
- Reclaim ownership over your body.
- Embrace being Black and sensitive.
- Practice radical honesty with yourself.
- And more…

There is endless joy that lives within you, and it is ready to be accessed and released. Self-care is an experience that is unique to each person, so no matter how you engage with the activities, there will be something that works for you in *Self-Care for Black Women*. It's time to lower your stress level, improve your overall wellness, and activate your Black Girl Magic. You ready? Let's go get 'em.

Why Black Women Must Practice Self-Care

*B*lack women are phenomenal. We come in different shapes, sizes, and shades. Some of us are mixed-race. Some of us have strong roots that are linked to Latin American countries, as well as the Caribbean. Some of us don't speak a lick of English. Some of us have skin color that is as dark as a vanilla bean or as light as cane sugar. Throughout history, Black women have been the glue in their communities. We provide physical and emotional support to families, friends, and strangers. We band together to uplift neighborhoods. We teach. We nurture. We build. And while we accomplish great things, we are being killed silently, because we do not practice proper self-care.

To be Black in this world is to constantly struggle. If you don't live with it, then you see it. And sometimes, you witness and experience it. It's a global struggle that started with the transatlantic slave trade and colonization. For centuries, Black people have been looked at as second-class citizens of the world. Used for our labor. Robbed of our identities. Gawked at for our unique features. And even though slavery was abolished, the societal system that was created as a result of white supremacy still exists to this day. Intergenerational trauma persists. This is trauma that was passed on from one generation to the next through learned behaviors and emotions. Understand this: The system was built to exhaust and exclude Black people. It was not built to help us win, which is why we—my sistahs—must look out for ourselves and each other.

Get ready to learn about how you can take care of your mind, body, and soul. Now more than ever, you must pour back into yourself what you so freely give to others. You will be introduced to topics like radical self-care (actively putting your wellness before others) and race-based traumatic stress (your body's response to mental and emotional damage). In addition, you will be given the tools to take back the power you need to put your wellness first.

The Reason for Self-Care

Ever feel overwhelmed, worn down, and burned out but you can't really identify the cause? Let me introduce you to something called race-based traumatic stress. The stress you experience related to racism is hurting your health—even the Centers for Disease Control and Prevention (CDC) confirmed it. Most health issues in Black women can be linked back to some form of racism. Whether it be on a personal or institutional level, racism is a proven risk factor for death in Black people. For example, racism attacks when your pleas for proper medical attention are ignored in the hospital. It attacks when you're sequestered into neighborhoods that lack proper resources. It attacks when you're not given the same life-altering opportunities as others. An overload of stress like this traumatically impacts your overall wellness. Your mind, body, and soul become so overwhelmed that these three vital areas of your life are unable to properly function. Hence, the need for self-care. Attending to yourself when you are experiencing traumatic stress is essential to maintaining your well-being.

What Is Race-Based Traumatic Stress?

Race-based traumatic stress was coined by Robert T. Carter, PhD. It describes your body's response to mental and emotional damage caused by negative race-related encounters, a.k.a. racism. Research has found that when you experience race-based traumatic stress, your body mimics the way it would react with post-traumatic stress disorder (PTSD).

This means that being on the receiving end of race-based discriminations, prejudice, hate crimes, or microaggressions can give you PTSD. Which means you have probably been walking around with a low-grade version of PTSD for many years, perhaps even decades. For instance, when you have paranoid or obsessive thoughts about how you should act to not be seen as a threat, that's PTSD. It throws off the functioning of your entire body.

The fact is, stress hurts. It leads to other debilitating diseases. And the hard truth is, racial stress kills. It leads to illnesses that cause death in your mind, body, and soul. With symptoms of PTSD, you become consumed by your perceived threat and are hyperfocused on keeping yourself safe. This makes it hard for you to simply enjoy life. However, no one has the time for that when we're just trying to survive being a Black woman in a racist and sexist society.

Self-Care in a Patriarchal Society

The stress that Black women experience from racism is combined with the stress of sexism. On top of racial trauma, Black women also have the pressure of dealing with being a woman in a patriarchal society, a "man's world." First the world tells you that you are less than because you're Black. And then it says, *Don't forget. You're a woman too.* You've got to act a certain way. You've got to meet unrealistic beauty standards. You can't get paid as much as men. And just as you settle into the complexities of your womanhood, you're reminded, *Don't forget. You're Black too.* It's a cycle that beats on your ability for self-care. Well, enough is enough. You know that systemic change is the key to full healing, but you need to take measures now to protect your well-being. You must bow out of the oppressive fight that is trying to kill you. It's time for you to regain control over your health. It's time to practice radical self-care.

What Is Radical Self-Care?

Radical self-care is the active decision to put your wellness before anyone or anything else. For Black women, it is a form of protest against a society that is determined to oppress us to death. By choosing to intentionally take care of yourself, you are letting the world know that you are a person who knows her worth and cannot be made a Black martyr. Radical self-care goes beyond your physical fitness. It also includes your emotional well-being, as well as the condition of your soul or spirit. This is called the mind-body-soul connection. Research has found that these three areas of your life are intertwined, so when one is acting up, it impacts the other two. Thus, you must learn when to use your radical self-care skills.

When to Use Radical Self-Care

Knowing when you need to use radical self-care is essential to your wellness. The answer? Every day. What makes radical self-care so different from other types of self-care is that it requires you to give your full attention to your well-being. Ever get a stomachache when you had to make a tough decision? Or when you were feeling extremely nervous? Or how about the time you said yes to something you didn't want to do? You know what I'm talking about. *Bubble guts.*

Bubble guts is an example of our mind, body, and soul talking to each other. Our spirit senses something isn't right, our mind is shooting out unhappy emotions, and our body is reacting as the stress hormones course through it. Incidents like this are signals that something is out of order within you, and that one of your needs must be addressed to maintain your health. To do this, maintaining balance within your three spheres of wellness is very important. You must use one of your acquired wellness tools. But real talk, that can be hard to do. Life happens. You get so distracted by the flow of your life that you forget to take care of yourself. Therefore, finding a practice of self-care that works for you is essential to the upkeep of your overall health.

How to Practice Radical Self-Care

To properly practice self-care, you must focus on all three areas: mind, body, and soul. Self-care is a set of daily practices that you do to support your well-being. These exercises, activities, or actions require you to put yourself first every day. Yes, girl. Every day. Self-care calls for you to get in touch with your inner being so you can learn what helps you cope in times of distress and what helps you create a life of happiness. Through self-care you gain knowledge on who you are as a person, allowing you to fall in love with the incredible woman you are on a daily basis.

The Purpose of Radical Self-Care

In addition, pursuing a life filled with self-care improves wellness and prevents illness and disease. The act of self-care has become critical to surviving in the modern world, especially as a Black woman. It helps you create a safe space for yourself in a society that does not care to make room for you. You help your future self and encourage personal growth when you engage in it. For you, self-care is a necessity and not a luxury.

Mental Self-Care

One of the most important areas to begin your focus of self-care is your mental health—the mind. This is the epicenter for your wellness. Your brain is a dynamic organ. It controls all the functions of your body. So much of how your brain operates dictates the person you become. Your memories, intelligence, and emotions are stored in your mind. From the time you're in the womb until you are in your late twenties, your brain is continually developing. What you go through in your childhood shapes the way you think, behave, and react. Through your family, you're introduced to things like love, self-worth, and conflict resolution. You may create unhealthy habits that were birthed from the early years of your brain development. You may even have traumatic experiences that alter the way you perceive people and things. But what is so fascinating about that brain of yours is that it has the capacity to reorganize what it has already learned.

Your brain has a characteristic called neuroplasticity. Neuroplasticity is your brain's ability to change and adapt the way it functions. This means that your mind is able to toss out things it's absorbed that no longer serve your well-being. Through emotional corrective experiences, like some of the self-care tips you'll explore in these pages, your brain can reroute you to a healthier way of thinking, and therefore living. This is so important for you. *It Is Necessary.* You can shake off your past, the old ways of thinking that have kept your mind captive, and chase after your own emotional wellness. Change the narrative of your life with self-love, and take on practices that purify and free your thoughts. Liberate your mind.

Physical Self-Care

The next area of focus for self-care is your physical health—the body. Your brain is not the only thing that remembers everything you experience in life. Your body also has its own memory bank. Good and bad emotions are stored in your body, especially unprocessed trauma. Your body also has a reaction to these different emotions. You might freeze when you get scared. You might get a headache when you're irritated. You might lose your appetite when you're feeling depressed. Taking care of your body requires you to listen to it and move it. You need

17

to pay attention to what that physical temple of yours is asking for. Is it nourishment? Is it pampering? Is it stillness? Is it action? Truly, moving your body is one of the best ways to take care of it. Things like stress and anxiety can paralyze us, creating bad habits that exacerbate whatever illnesses are trying to take root in our bodies. And as a strong Black woman, you may have been taught to ignore your physical pains, to disregard what your body is trying to tell you. Well, that stops here. It's time to give your body the love and respect it deserves.

Spiritual Self-Care

The last focus of self-care is your spiritual health—your soul. This is the essence of who you are on the inside. Tending to your spiritual life doesn't necessarily mean practicing religion. It can include your faith, but it's about taking care of your inner being, your higher self—who is connected to the universe around it. Soul self-care encompasses activities that help you tap deeper into parts of you beyond your mind and body, like your intuition. Taking care of your spirit is what helps keep you motivated to pursue total healing. You will feel more connected to the world and humanity. This self-love practice guides you to your life's purpose. It helps you walk and live in that fulfillment. It's what fills you up with peace beyond understanding.

Self-care for your soul is essential. The more you take care of your soul, the more you get comfortable with who you are as a person. The world around you is always trying to tell you who you should be or what you should look like as a Black woman. Your consciousness gets clouded by the stress and trauma from attempting to just be. In most spaces, you aren't allowed to be your full self. Spiritual self-care is where you get to unabashedly tap into the magic being inside of you. You get to say hello to her and get to know her intimately. Love gently on your soul, so it can be the guiding light you need.

Choose Yourself

Ultimately, self-care is healing work for your entire being. From your mind, to your body, and to your soul, the self-care activities you use to take care of yourself can overlap. Because that's the goal: total healing of your personhood. When you heal yourself, you create an earth-shattering legacy. The lineage of women who come after you will be healed. Your inner circle of Black women around you, healed.

By actively choosing yourself, you are breaking the generational curses or traumas that have cycled through your family. You activate your ancestral strength. Things like addiction and abuse, they stop with you. You change the way children in your bloodline will be raised. You break down emotional barriers that no longer keep feelings like fear and shame imprisoned in your body. You bend the universe with the powerful stomp of your walk to a higher level of self-worth. You create an exceptional example for yourself and others of what self-love truly means. You teach yourself and the next generations about the importance of their own self-care. Radical self-care is a movement that you cannot let pass you by. You must participate. The world depends on it. You depend on it.

Part 1
MIND

The suggested exercises in this section will require you to be intentional, dig deep, and have fun. They are designed to lead you back to you: the keeper of your emotional wellness. You will be asked to reflect on your feelings and thoughts, tapping into total awareness of what's going on in your head. You may even be triggered by some of these activities, which is when you experience a strong emotional response. This is good. Self-care for your mind requires a healthy emotional release as you face hard truths about yourself. It's all about gathering you and your mental health together.

Some tips are everyday suggested actions you've probably heard of before. Other exercises are those only someone like you—a Black woman—will benefit from. Most importantly, with whichever activities you decide to incorporate into your daily life, you will be doing one special thing: choosing yourself. Let's do this!

Take a Deep Breath

Throughout the day, our fight, flight, freeze mode—or stress response—is activated. Like that time your white coworker asked to touch your hair, *as they were touching it*. You had to dig deep into your soul to not do something that would land you in the unemployment line. Or, that time you heard someone who was not Black use the N-word. Oh wait, and how about that time when someone said you were "pretty for a Black girl." You get it. People try Black women, every day.

These incidents are called microaggressions—daily slights or insults that intentionally or unintentionally put down someone of a marginalized group. It's like death by a thousand bee stings; one negative comment hurts, but to constantly experience them is deadly for your psyche.

When experiencing these incidents, which often bring on anxiety, one of the most powerful tools to use is your breath. Often, when we are distressed, we are breathing improperly. We might be holding our breath or breathing rapidly. Taking a moment to practice a breathing exercise will help you slow down your breath and let go of the stress you're carrying, signaling to your brain and body to calm down. Here's how to get back to a steady breath: Inhale through your nose for five seconds and exhale out your mouth for five seconds, or until all the air is out of your lungs. If needed, add in a deep sigh as you breathe out. This can be done once throughout the day or repeated as you sit for a longer period.

Experiencing microaggressions every day weighs heavily on you. You need to let go of your feelings tied to them; they are not for you to carry. The racially rude things people say to you are not a reflection of your worth. Take a moment right now to think about your most recent interaction that left you questioning the magnificence of your existence as a Black woman. Take one deep breath and exhale, releasing any anger and pain you are holding on to from this experience. You should feel lighter with a clearer mind as you better navigate your road to radical self-care.

Release Feelings of Guilt Around Self-Love

As you do the work to improve your well-being, feelings of guilt may arise. You're not alone. This is a common experience among Black women. Often, society makes us feel like we are not deserving of the good things that come to us—unless we worked tirelessly to get them. We are conditioned to push forward through bad feelings, ignoring signs of depression and anxiety to take care of everyone else. So when you put your wellness above others, you feel guilty. *claps* *Aht, aht.* It's time to release those feelings of guilt around practicing radical self-care to become a better, healthier you.

Grab a notebook and do the following: Begin with evaluating where these emotions are coming from. Take some time to think and ask yourself: *Where did I learn that I should put the needs of others before mine? Why do I think I must justify my requirement of self-care?* Next, apologize to yourself for the times you pushed yourself beyond your limits and ignored your need for self-love. Follow up with forgiving the origin of the guilt. It is most likely a woman caregiver (maybe a mom or grandma) who didn't provide you with a good example of what caring for yourself should look like. She did the best she could with the amount of awareness she had of herself. Most importantly, commit to not judging yourself if feelings of guilt arise as you practice self-care.

Ultimately, the more you work on not feeling guilty about taking care of yourself, the closer you get to experiencing the freedom you deserve.

Write in a Journal

Simply existing in this world as a Black woman is traumatic. One of the best ways to process all the things swirling around in your head is to write in a journal. Creating time in your day to scribble down what's going on in your mind has many benefits. By keeping a journal filled with your thoughts, feelings, and experiences, you will be making room for yourself to have emotional breakthroughs, find healing, gain self-confidence, and build self-awareness. Let's keep it real: You need to cultivate this space for yourself. No one else will. The bottled-up emotions that you are carrying must make their way onto paper. It will help reduce any obsessive thinking and unpleasant feelings.

Make journaling worth it by doing any of the following: Jot down your goals for the year and revisit them in six months. Carve out ten to fifteen minutes before bed to write about your day, detailing things that happened and how you felt. Write down your dreams from the night before when you first wake up. Purchase a journal with prompts that will force you to reflect on your thoughts and behaviors. Any of the aforementioned journaling techniques will help make the experience fun for you.

Now is the time to get a journal if you don't own one already. Use your computer or phone if handwriting your thoughts is not your thing. You need it to step up your mental wellness. Challenge yourself to write and push through any barriers you might be facing on your journey to radical self-care. Your breakthrough is waiting. Let the pages lead you.

Ignore Your Phone in the Morning

Most people start their morning by looking at their smartphones. However, is it healthy for our brains to engage in the large world that exists in our palm, as soon as we wake? No, ma'am. It is not. Here's a way to avoid checking your phone before you rise and shine: Get an alarm clock. You know, an actual alarm clock that isn't connected to your phone. Then—and this is the key—charge your phone away from the bed. Choose a location that requires you to get up, like in the kitchen. This will help you curb the habit of reaching for it first thing.

All in all, making this small change will improve your mental state. You'll have more peaceful mornings and start your day with a clear head and elevated mood, since there are many reasons why including cellphones in your morning ritual is detrimental to your mental health. First off, it's not good for your eyes. The blue light your phone emits strains them. Why start the morning with a headache? Second, you are flooding your brain with too much information too early. Checking emails and social media while you're still in bed increases anxiety and stress. You could go from having sweet dreams to immediately being annoyed about a work-related email or a video of Karen not minding her own business (a.k.a. carin' 'bout the wrong thing). Third, it might trigger other unhealthy emotions like envy when you start your day scrolling other people's timelines. Put the phone down. Think about your radical self-care goals.

Challenge Your Negative Self-Talk

How we speak to ourselves impacts our mental health. This is why you must challenge any negative self-talk immediately. Self-talk is what is considered our internal voice. It speaks to us throughout the day as we maneuver different situations. However, sometimes, our thoughts lean toward the negative side as they're impacted by our experiences and beliefs. Such as being conditioned as a Black woman by your surroundings to believe your skin, hair, and body are less than desirable. They're not, by the way. You are beautiful. We subconsciously pick up these messages and start to tell ourselves things like *I am not good enough. I can't seem to get anything right. I will never find love. No one wants a woman who looks like me.*

Girl, stop. Thinking like this will only lead to increased feelings of stress and sadness. You are good enough.

The next time you realize you are talking badly about yourself, interrupt those thoughts with positive self-talk and some reality testing. This is when you examine your thoughts and perceptions to see if they match your external world. Be objective and ask yourself: *What evidence do I have to back up my thinking? What would happen to my feelings and actions if I changed my thoughts?* Disrupting negative self-talk is how you gain power over your mental wellness and enhance your radical self-care.

Needless to say, this exercise should decrease your negative thoughts and improve your mood. You should begin to feel better and believe your positive self-talk the more you practice.

Stop Pursuing Perfectionism

When's the last time you failed beautifully at something? Didn't set any performance expectations for it and just rolled with it? The fact is: Black women are naturally high achievers. Statistically, we earn the most degrees in higher education. We are out here racking up diplomas, small businesses, and other goals. The world expects us to fail, so we go hard. And as a high achiever, you've probably accomplished great things by doing it your way, so you think you can't trust anyone because you're the only person with common sense and competence at your workplace, in your home, and everywhere else! *Whew.*

Really, pursuing perfectionism is just anxiety acting up. Being a perfectionist is also about shielding yourself—*cough* ego *cough*—from getting hurt. Choosing perfectionism is also about holding your emotions hostage, because you don't trust yourself to handle any unforeseen blowbacks. Or, you're afraid to make mistakes. Too much? Still reading? I'm not trying to drag you, sis. Just telling the truth.

To break this habit, you'll need to try any of the following: Embrace your mistakes and resist the need to judge yourself; allow yourself to try something new and fail as you learn; and ask for help with a task without dictating its execution. It will be hard, but you can do it. Take time to look for opportunities to just be okay on your radical self-care discovery.

Ultimately, it'll feel weird at first, but eventually you'll be free of anxiety, self-judgment, and the need to be perfect.

Vent to a Friend Who Validates You

Sometimes it can feel like our experiences in this world do not matter. You may feel invisible or unnoticed, as if no one cares about your existence. The strange thing about being a Black woman is that we're visible, but our humanity can be invisible. And when we're going through life feeling like no one cares about our problems, suppressing and ignoring our feelings is inevitable. However, this is not good. Pushing down your emotions can lead to misdirected anger, increased feelings of stress, and the use of unhealthy coping skills. You need to be able to let out your frustrations in a healthy space. One of the best ways to do this is with a friend you trust—specifically, a pal who validates your existence.

Start by ensuring they have space for you to vent. Let 'em know you need to talk and ask if they have the emotional capacity to listen. Next, tell them you are just looking to be heard and validated, not challenged. Afterward, thank them for taking the time to hear you out. Most importantly, make sure you return the favor when they're in need of the same.

Ultimately, it's important for you to have a friend who, when you say, "My job got me messed up," their response is "Tell me what happened." They simply agree with your current emotions and act as a soft sounding board for you to say whatever is on your mind. Treasure this friend for being part of your radical self-care experience.

Do a Grounding Exercise

Sometimes it feels like the world requires so much from us yet refuses to give us any assistance or leniency. This can be overwhelming as a Black woman. Trying to dodge stereotypes and unrealistic expectations of how we should be moving through life is stressful. It can cause serious bouts of anxiety and internal pressure that make it hard for us to think or function. If you find yourself having one of these moments, try this grounding exercise. This activity can be done anywhere and anytime.

- **Locate *five* things you can see.** Take time to look around and spot items you see in your surroundings, such as a crack in the wall.
- **Notice *four* things you can touch.** Feel the sensation of things that are in contact with your body, like this book you're holding. *wink*
- **Recognize *three* things you can hear.** Point out noises your mind has tuned out—for example, the sound of a fan blowing.
- **Find *two* things you can smell.** Pay attention to fragrances near you or look around for something with a scent.
- **Identify *one* thing you can taste.** Pop a mint in your mouth or take a sip of water to complete this activity.

The goal of this activity is to help you regain control of your emotions and distract your mind from what is causing you distress. You should feel more relaxed after completing all five steps. Remember, your radical self-care journey is all about you. Wherever you are, whatever you're doing, stop for a moment and take it all in.

Mourn Your Losses

To grieve is to mourn the loss of something or someone. Bereavement is an important process in times of death, change, and trauma. Our minds need this restorative time. In the Black community, we do not only mourn the loss of lives from people we personally know. We mourn the loss of innocent Black lives due to police brutality and other race-related tragedies (#SayHerName). We mourn the loss of our ability to be seen for our humanity. We mourn the loss of a deeper connection to our ancestral roots. We mourn the loss of our individuality, as society insists on lumping the Black experience into one. The fact is, grief is not linear. It comes and goes in waves. And like an onion, with every new layer peeled, there is something to address.

Foremost, you must know the five stages of grief: denial, anger, bargaining, depression, and acceptance. Often, you may find yourself bypassing these stages to ignoring your emotions. Or, you might get stuck somewhere between anger and depression. Evaluate where you are mentally when you experience any kind of loss and do the following: Acknowledge your emotions. Allow yourself to feel whatever comes up without judgment, release your feelings in a safe space (perhaps with a trusted friend or in your journal), and resist putting a time limit on your grieving process.

Overall, mourning losses is an important activity to integrate into self-care routines. It softens the blows that come with life adjustments. Most importantly, you give yourself permission to honor what was lost and create space to move forward.

Heal Your Inner Child

How many times were you silenced as a child? How many times were your emotional or physical needs ignored when you were young? How many times did you have to take responsibility for the feelings and actions of the adults around you? Too many to count, right? *I feel you, girl.*

Sometimes self-care can get messy and painful. And, well, this is one of those activities. You may not want to do it, but you *have* to. Radical self-care is calling, and your peace of mind is waiting. Addressing unresolved childhood trauma is vital to our personal growth. Period. You need to do this to elevate your mind to the next level. No matter your age, the little girl in you is potentially hurting and acting out as an adult and needs to find healing.

So what does it mean to heal your inner child? This kind of self-care involves deepening your self-awareness to treat mental traumas, unlearn dysfunctional habits, and correct self-sabotaging behaviors. You essentially reparent the little girl inside of you. The one who didn't receive the kind of nurturing you required to assist you in developing healthy habits.

Healing your inner child is especially important for Black women. Studies have revealed that in and outside the classroom, young Black girls are seen and treated as adults. *Tuh.* Little Black girls are robbed of their childhood innocence. The consequences for the inevitable oopsies that Black kids make (because they are children and children mess up **eyeroll**) are far greater than those of children from any other race.

This is a heavy exercise, so please go at a pace that works for you. You may feel sad and overwhelmed afterward. However, trust that the longer you practice this ongoing activity, the sooner you will begin to feel healed. You can start here: Treat yourself as if you are your own parent. In moments of distress, ask yourself, *What do I need in this moment right now, and how can I get it for myself?* And as you continue to reparent, visualize yourself as a little girl. Hug her. Let her cry in your arms and mourn the childhood you wish she could've had. Tell her that anything she experienced in her childhood that hurt her was not her fault. Make a promise to that little girl that you will do whatever you can to take care of her.

Make sure you find a way to treat yourself after doing this hard work. You deserve it. So does your inner child who needs you to be well. Your radical self-care is her radical self-care. The sooner you start, the better you both will be.

Embrace Being Black and Sensitive

Are you sensitive to certain sounds, smells, and noises? Do you feel like you absorb the information in your surroundings and then need time to observe and process before acting? Well, girl, you might be one of the 20 percent of the population who is a highly sensitive person (HSP). This is a real thing that you should discuss with a mental health professional. *I can't diagnose you through this book.* However, if you really feel like this is you, then all it means is you have a special power: a deeper sense of awareness and empathy than most people. Being able to feel deeply is a gift that should be embraced.

If you suspect you might be an HSP, begin by becoming aware of when you experience sensory overload. If you feel overwhelmed, take some time to recuperate. Release any judgment you may have around being sensitive. Use this newfound superpower to help inform the actions you take to practice self-care. Hopefully, you'll have a better understanding of your needs.

Nonetheless, let's get down to "sensitive" and "Black" being in the same sentence. We are not given the space to be vulnerable. The "strong Black woman" trope is given to us by others, and we sometimes wear it with a badge of honor. Proud of how much suffering we can take and still thrive. A Black martyr. For whose benefit, though? Sure ain't yours. Even if you don't fully identify as an HSP, toss out the need to always be a superwoman. Step into radical self-care by embracing sensitivity as a strength and not a weakness.

Stop Policing Your Speech

We are conditioned to be superconscious of how we speak. With hypervisibility as a Black woman comes hyperawareness. Of how you sound, how you look, how you eat, how you walk, how you breathe. It's exhausting. We try to not feed into the "angry Black woman" stereotype, so we purposefully speak lower and softer when we'd rather be a bit louder and more direct. We adjust our tone so we don't offend others by possibly coming off as aggressive. We withhold words because we fear that if we say something, we will be vilified. We hold the weight of speaking for all Black women with our voices, when we just want to speak for ourselves. Whew. Girl. It's time to cut this behavior and take back your voice.

To stop policing your speech, try the following: First, actively work on letting go of fear and doubt of being misunderstood. Some people are determined to misconstrue what you say simply because you're Black. Forget those folks. Second, if you feel like you are coming from a good place, say it all with your chest. Third, find small opportunities, like with a trusted friend, to convey exactly how you're feeling without adjusting your tone. Say what you need to say without second-guessing yourself.

As you practice this activity, you'll begin to let go of obsessive thoughts and gain the self-confidence necessary to continue your road to radical self-care. You will find your voice again and not be afraid to use it, despite what others may think of you.

Set Boundaries with Yourself

Let's talk about setting boundaries with yourself. Often, boundaries are talked about in the context of something we do to save ourselves from other people's behavior. Surprise: Boundary setting starts with you creating boundaries to protect your mental peace and emotional capacity. People and things will try to tap into your energy tank and drain it. You must set rules and regulations for yourself to prevent an increase in stress, depression, anxiety, and other mental health symptoms. Boundaries allow you to create a life that is yours. A life that is worth living. A life that is wonderfully made how you imagined it. Boundaries are not for others. *Read that again.* Boundaries are not for others.

Sometimes, as a Black woman, you might find it hard to set boundaries because you are not used to getting to put your needs first. You might care too much about offending others or appearing weak-minded. Let it go. Creating boundaries with yourself is one of the strongest things you can do. You are honoring yourself by doing this, and you are teaching others that you matter too.

How to set boundaries with yourself: Peep what's exhausting you. Whether it's a person (*cough* *that f-boy you just can't quit* *cough*) or a habit, if it's bringing your energy levels down, begin thinking about what limits you can set for yourself. *whispers* *Delete and block his number.*

Don't allow yourself to succumb to the stresses of the world. Create boundaries that lead to even more radical self-care.

Process Racism Encounters with a Safe Person

It's important to locate people with whom you can process the racism you experience. This could be a Black friend or anyone who *gets it*. This person will not try to convince you that you didn't experience racism. They'll say *I get it* when you tell them you were told, "This is first class," as you clutched your first-class ticket. They'll say *I understand* when you tell them no one wanted to sit next to you on a crowded bus or train, despite the empty seat next to you being the only one available. They'll say *I gotchu* when you tell them about how no one listens to your idea in a meeting unless it's repeated by one of your white coworkers.

You deserve a space where you can let out the ugly feelings associated with experiencing racism. Those emotions are not yours to hold on to. Being denied the validity of encountering racism is gaslighting—when you are told something that forces you to question your own reality and intuition. Like, "Oh, do you really think they did that because you're Black?" People who gaslight you are damaging to your psyche and self-perspective. You'll know by the way they react to your encounters with racism. At the first sight of any invalidation of your feelings, run. Find safe people and let it out.

It's time to take back your mental and emotional freedom, and that freedom starts with the idea that you are not the problem. You are the solution.

Create Boundaries at Work

Let's talk about the workplace. Depending on where you work, you might be the only one or one of the few Black women at your job. Let us take a moment to pray for your sanity. If this is not you, and you somehow work at a place where there are many people who look like you, please let a girl know where she can send her resume. Otherwise, learn to create boundaries at work that protect your peace.

Here's what creating boundaries at work can look like. First off, do not engage with *that* problematic coworker unless it is work-related. Seriously. Leave Becky and her racially ignorant self alone. Next, identify a work buddy at your job who doesn't require you to suppress your Blackness. This may take some time, but be open to the possibility that there is someone at your job who understands your plight in the workplace. Additionally, address work concerns with your supervisor when you feel like you are being mistreated. Unfair increased workload? Speak up, immediately. You deserve an amount of work that is of realistic proportions. Lastly, embrace healthy code-switching. The greatest thing about being a Black woman is that you know how to adapt to any situation. As long as you are not hiding parts of your identity that are tied to your Blackness, then go ahead. Use that professional voice of yours without shame.

To put it plainly: Being the token Black woman at your job sucks. *Sucks.* It is tiring. The environment some of us work in mimics the structures of institutional racism. We are given a seat at the table, but not given a meal. We have to work twice as hard to get half the recognition of our non–Black coworkers. We are constantly having to manage the hypervisibility of our Blackness by our colleagues, especially our boss. *Can I wear my natural hair? Should I be working harder? Do I sound mean, angry, or intimidating? Am I not getting promoted because I'm Black?* It's maddening. These anxious thoughts can distract you from doing your job. You know, the one where it seems like you are required to do a lot more labor than other folks....*side-eye* That's why it is important to create boundaries at work.

Exercising these boundaries will help prevent you from experiencing higher levels of frustration and burnout within the workplace on your journey to radical self-care. You will be set up for success, keeping you motivated at your job. Creating healthy work boundaries will allow you to actually work.

Watch Others Protest on Social Media

You are your own cause. Your journey to wellness is your most important fight. Therefore, attending a protest is not the only way to fight against racial injustice. Here are some ways you can actively watch others protest on social media: like, comment on, and share content from those who are protesting. Or, donate to any fund that goes toward an organization or person who is assisting in organizing a protest. Ultimately, you can support our people without leaving the comfort of your house.

Remember, self-care is a form of resistance. If being part of a large gathering that is marching through the streets gives you anxiety, sit this one out. It can get real dicey out in those streets while protesting, so only go if you feel you can mentally handle what is to come from the experience. Like, getting arrested…because when Black people protest, the government calls every police officer on their payroll to harass those in the streets. Even when it's a peaceful protest. *Hmph.* We don't need to go to a protest to prove anything about our Blackness. We don't need to attend a protest to show we believe Black Lives Matter. You living your life is enough proof of these things. Taking this approach will help you feel like you are part of the movement without disrupting your mental peace. Just remember to limit your online activity.

Read Something for Fun

When's the last time you read something simply for your own enjoyment? You know, where you purposefully carved out time so you could get lost in a book of your choice? *Sit and read for an hour or two?! Who has the time?!*

From fiction to nonfiction, there are many genres of books. Start engaging in reading for fun by first figuring out what kind will leave you feeling energized when you're done with it. Creating time to read will help us find an escape from everyday stressors and the coping defenses created by them. Like the heaviness in our mind from the mental gymnastics of managing our existence as a Black woman, trying to be understood without intimidating others. We need to reclaim our time and our minds.

Make time to find something you like, then buy or borrow from the library a physical or digital copy of what you've decided to read and enjoy it. Pay attention to details, like unfamiliar words, the location of the page numbers, and the feeling of the pages. This is all part of your mental escape

In short, what makes reading so good for our mind is that it is a mindfulness activity that encourages us to stay present and release any self-judgment, with the focus being on the activity we're doing. Put down your phone and stop digesting the details of the latest shooting-related death of an unarmed Black man. Please. It's too much. You deserve a much-needed break.

Literally, start a new chapter and put your mind at ease.

Check In with Your Thoughts

To do a self-check with your mind, grab a notebook. Now answer these questions, and reflect on them: *What are my thoughts right now? How do these thoughts impact my mood? When did I start thinking about these things? How often am I thinking about them? Who is a safe person that I can share my thoughts with today?* The purpose of this activity is to become more in tune with your mental wellness. Your answers to these questions will increase your self-awareness.

Let's spend some time checking in with our thoughts. Our minds deserve some extra tender loving care. As a Black woman, you may not feel comfortable attending to your own needs, thereby working twice as hard to not be stereotyped as lazy. You take care of others and neglect your emotional needs in the midst of it. You gotta stop this. We deserve a mind filled with clarity. And when it comes to our thoughts, there are specific things we need to assess to make sure our mind is operating at its healthiest. Checking in with your thoughts is like taking your mind to the mental mechanic. There is no reason to crash and burn. Regular tune-ups are a necessity. After doing this, you'll feel more equipped with how to properly take care of your mental health on the road to radical self-care discovery.

Resist Being the Token Black Girl

If you grew up as one of the few, if not only, Black girls in your school, then you know the struggle of being the Token Black Girl, a.k.a. TBG. Side effects of being the TBG may include feelings of responsibility for the perception of your race, behaving as a cultural liaison or translator for your non-Black friends, ignoring racist jokes to maintain friendships, and unknowingly acquiring feelings of internalized racism. The last symptom is the absolute worst. It creates self-hate for yourself and your kinfolk. Being a TBG is the breeding ground for impostor syndrome and normalizing invalidating our misogynoir experiences. It's not good for our mental health. You must try to avoid being the Token Black Girl at all costs.

To resist being the TBG, start by forgiving yourself for the times you behaved in a way that betrayed your true identity. You were just trying to survive and fit in. That's okay. Next and most importantly, find friends who don't put you in this role. You can always adjust your friend group. Don't be afraid to make a change. Overall, the benefits of not being a TBG are beneficial to your mental health.

Your radical self-care is an endless opportunity of alternate endings. Go learn your own unique identity. You are a dynamic human being with an intricate story that is still unfolding. Yes, being Black is a part of that, but that's not all you are.

Find a Black Woman Therapist

A therapist is a licensed mental health professional who can guide us through our thoughts, feelings, and actions. They are people, *like ya girl who wrote this book,* who are clinically trained to assist you in decluttering your mind, creating effective coping skills, and furthering any personal goals. So, having a therapist who looks like you is critical to your mental health.

In your therapeutic relationship, you will also find self-love—discovering who you truly are, gaining the power to listen to your own intuition, and empowering yourself to action in the name of self-care. You will also uncover past or current trauma in a safe space so that you can examine how it impacts your decisions, behaviors, and relationships. Most importantly, a therapist is a human like you who has experienced similar trials and tribulations as you, and if your therapist is Black and female, she can relate culturally. It's a whole new level of personal healing, sis. *This* is the type of person you want knowing the intimate details of your life. Access, availability, and stigma are barriers to finding a Black woman therapist. However, it is possible.

How to find a Black woman therapist:

- **Determine what you want to get out of therapy.** It can be simply having a space to talk or tackle something specific like depression. You don't need to have a mental illness to seek out support from a therapist.
- **If you have health insurance, you can reach out to them and request assistance with locating a Black therapist.**

Most insurance companies have an online database of their mental health providers. Take time to research and reach out to each professional you're interested in seeing.

- **Find a mental health professional through an online directory.** If you're in the United States, try Psychology Today, Black Female Therapists, Inclusive Therapists, and Therapy for Black Girls. If you're in the United Kingdom, try the British Association for Counselling and Psychotherapy, Self Space, and the United Kingdom Council for Psychotherapy.
- **Consider trying different therapists before you decide on one.** It's all about finding a mental health provider that fits.

Overall, finding a Black woman therapist will change your life. If you've never been to therapy before, give it a try. Be patient with the process, as it'll probably feel out of your comfort zone to share your business with a stranger. However, recognize that this is a new relationship, and eventually your therapist will be an integral part of your mental wellness. A new level of personal growth awaits. Reach it with a Black woman therapist who can lead the way to the radical self-care you deserve.

Create a Vision Board

Get crafty and intentional with your life by creating a vision board—a powerful mental exercise tool that will allow you to visualize and manifest your goals. To our mind, seeing is believing. Literally. It's been discovered that when we imagine ourselves doing something, the same memory registers in our body. So if we think about our goals, we subconsciously make steps toward achieving them. The benefit of making a vision board is that your focus and confidence will increase. You'll get to visualize how you see yourself as a Black woman, not how the world sees you. Additionally, your motivation to hit your goals will skyrocket. If this entices you, then you need to complete this self-care activity.

Decide what type of board you will use. It could be a poster board, a piece of cardboard, or a corkboard, whatever works for you. Next, reflect on what you want on your vision board. Grab some magazines or print out images, quotes, etc. Then choose things that will make you feel good and align with your life's intention. Now secure everything on your board however you decide, and place your vision board somewhere you will always see it. Look at it every day and manifest your best life.

As you take in your vision board daily, you will feel inspired. You may notice feelings of anxiety disappear as you start to believe what you see. If you can see it, you can achieve it. Believe that something better awaits you on your journey to radical self-care, and see yourself well.

Cut Off Emotionally Immature People

Cutting off people who are bad for your mental health can feel painful. It's severing a bond with someone. And while initially it will hurt, over time you will experience the benefits of no longer engaging in a toxic relationship. This is critical to your own journey of radical self-care.

Here are some signs of someone with poor emotional maturity: First, they go from zero to 100 *real* quick. They lack the ability to self-regulate, effectively communicate, and resolve conflict calmly. Second, they are unable to be held accountable and blame others for their actions or get defensive about their negative behaviors. Third, they can't see beyond themselves. Basically, a narcissist. And fourth, they don't respect your boundaries or try to convince you to move them.

To cut these people off, let go of any responsibility you may be holding regarding their emotions. You are not responsible for how anyone feels or behaves. You are only responsible for yourself. In addition, decide how and when you will disengage with them. It can be sudden or gradual. You decide, as people who lack emotional maturity are energy suckers. This doesn't mean they are bad people. It means their behaviors are toxic and wreak havoc on your psyche. This type of person could be a family member, a friend, a lover, a coworker, etc. You'll know you're in the presence of an emotionally immature person based on your feelings after the interaction. Are you feeling confused, exhausted, or annoyed? If so, it's time to cut them off.

Take a Break from Your Healing

Our need to be productive should not include our healing work. Just like cuts need time to heal without being further irritated, so do our emotions. Yes, we are a work in progress, but we do not need to be a building always under construction. Create time to just be. Walk in the new enlightenments you have encountered through your acts of self-care. Practice your newfound self-love. Taking a break releases any self-judgments about how you should act or think as a Black woman. It is essential to any work we are doing, especially mental.

Fall back, relax, and settle into the current you. Here's how:

- **Put down the self-help books.** (*Not this one!*) Stop reading anything that picks at your internal wounds, triggering trauma responses—like overreaction to something that reminds you of a past hurt. You are reacting to a previous trauma and not the current situation.
- **Learn your triggers and stay away from them.** If you're tired of dealing with microaggressions, particularly from white people, regularly avoid situations where you interact intimately with them. Engaging in a way that honors and protects your sanity with people who hit you with racial or sexist slights daily is an act of healing at work.
- **Mute self-help *Instagram* pages periodically.** The content is often great, but you don't need to be encouraged every day to improve your mind and address your issues.

Taking breaks from our healing is about survival. It is exhausting to tackle emotional concerns every chance we get.

Let Go of Impostor Syndrome

Impostor syndrome can strike at any moment. It is very common among Black women. Indicators of impostor syndrome include questioning the validity of our successes, feeling like we don't belong, worrying about being exposed as a fraud for our accomplishments, and doubting our own talents. Sound familiar? Mhm, thought so. The most common place to experience this is at work or school. We're surrounded by individuals who already make us question our worth or existence, so it would make sense that we too would begin to believe we are undeserving of our wins. Nah. Stop that right now. You deserve any and every goal you hit. But in the moment, while experiencing victory, it can feel like you shouldn't be victorious. Here are some ways to let go of impostor syndrome.

First, create a jar or box of wins. Whenever you accomplish something, write it down and toss it in. When impostor syndrome strikes, look back and remind yourself you're *that* girl. Second, connect with a friend who knows all of your business. This person can remind you of your journey to success, encouraging you to reminisce about the hard work you put in to get to where you are. And third, give impostor syndrome a name. Whenever she appears, tell her to sit her butt down as you make boss-like moves.

It's important you shake off impostor syndrome because it might hold you back from experiencing the fullness of the accomplishments you deserve. Radical self-care will help you to see yourself as you truly are. Celebrate.

Accept That Multiple Truths Can Coexist

Absolute thinking is unhealthy for our mind. This is when we create beliefs and thoughts that things are very concrete, all or nothing. Like, believing we must be married and have children by a certain age. *Stares at the media who is always telling Black women we are the least desirable.* Not allowing multiple truths to exist in our mind hinders our ability to emotionally regulate ourselves, and it can even prevent us from achieving our goals. We get so caught up in the idea that something must be done one way to achieve a specific outcome that we don't allow ourselves to explore other routes.

Here are some ways you can embrace multiple truths: When you feel like you are engaging in absolute thinking, try asking yourself, *Is there another way this could turn out? Is there another way to do this?* And when you have several emotions moving through you that feel contradictory to each other, allow yourself to experience them.

When it comes to our emotions, we are allowed to have multiple feelings about something. You can be sad that a toxic relationship is over, but still miss the person. Multiple truths are allowed to coexist. It just means you are a normal, dynamic human being with many emotions.

As you practice this activity, you will feel less anxious and more empowered to achieve your goals. You let go of your need to control, understanding that many roads can lead you to the same destination of radical self-care.

Do Nothing for Twenty Minutes

Okay, girl. Let's hit the reset button. After a long day or week, sitting and doing nothing for twenty minutes will feel like taking a deep breath of fresh air. The world around us is chaotic and moving fast. We're being asked to give so much of ourselves at work and in our personal life. (Sigh. Black girl problems.) We need a quiet moment like this to ourselves. Hit the pause button on your brain. You need to be reminded to slow down and breathe. This activity will allow you to calm the chatter floating through your mind, as well as decrease your levels of anxiety and stress. Take twenty minutes to reset, then continue about the business of managing your radical self-care discovery.

Some ways to do nothing for twenty minutes: Turn on your favorite playlist or album, sit or lie down, and stare at the ceiling as you vibe out to your favorite songs. Sit or lie down and focus on your breath. If you do this one right, you might just fall asleep for a catnap. Lie on your bed and run through your wins for the day or week. Obviously, you can enjoy your twenty minutes of mental freedom however you see fit. Give it a try and see what happens.

51

Mind Your Business

Minding our business is one of the best things we can do for our mental health. Seriously. Sometimes, we feel like we must insert ourselves into somebody else's mess under the guise of helping. But really, all we're doing is attempting to control the outcome of their actions. Sis, that ain't nothing but you projecting your lifestyle choices onto another. That is you thinking you know better what those individuals need for themselves. Needing to scoot your way into someone's business is also you trying to work through your own anxiety and fear with whatever that person has going on in their life. Sometimes Black women do this to each other under the guise of "looking out for a sistah." Good sentiment, but you wouldn't want anybody in your business. So, it's time to let people be.

When you feel yourself poking your nose in other people's business, try this: Repeat to yourself: *That's not my business. That's not my business.* Embrace the truth that there is more than one way of doing things. Unless they're specifically asking for your opinion, that's not your business.

Whether they are a person in your life or someone you're gawking at on social media, let them be. Shift that energy and focus on yourself as you navigate your own journey to radical self-care. You will feel ten times less anxious and more motivated to work toward your goals because all your attention is on the most important person you know: yourself.

Embrace Your Bad Days

It would be nice if every day was a super-duper awesome day. However, that's not reality. The fact is that we all have bad days. We have days where a boss, a family member, or a friend really ticks us off. And that coupled with daily microaggressions? *Whew.* Horrible combo. Feel encouraged to grab hold of those days and give yourself permission to experience those negative feelings. Self-love isn't always about fishing for the good vibes. It's about honoring yourself. If you were to lie to yourself and simply brush off your bad day, you would be suppressing your true emotions, and thus dishonoring your inner being. The key to doing this is not allowing your bad day to ruin someone else's great day. You are responsible for your own emotions.

Start by acknowledging that you had a crappy day. Phone a friend and vent. You're allowed to say out loud that your day sucks. Saying this loosens the hold on the emotions that the stressor is keeping captive. Embracing bad days is actually really good for our mind. Follow up with releasing the idea that your bad day was your fault. Sometimes, things happen and there are no reasons. Do not force yourself to make sense of it. Let go and think about how you can take care of yourself. Feelings fade. Your bad day will pass.

After you embrace your bad day, you won't instantly feel better. But you will feel relieved that you gave yourself permission to honor your true feelings on your road to radical self-care.

Stop Educating People on Racism

Talking about racism is hard. Living through racism is painful. The burden of concerns related to diversity, equity, and inclusion seems to always fall on the shoulders of nonwhites. Especially Black women. We are often tasked with the hard labor of sharing our race-related traumas while creating solutions to fix the system that created racism. *Make it make sense.* And as more people seem to become aware of their own racial bias and ignorance, we may also be asked to educate folks on how they can be anti-racist. Don't do it. It's not your job to teach someone how to see Black people as human beings. It's not your job to provide someone with the resources to not judge your skin color. It's not your job to teach people how to be better humans. You may find it tempting to help those who are trying to be less racist, but honey, the emotional labor that comes with this kind of personal work is excessive. Stop trying to teach them.

First off, release any responsibility you feel you have with educating non-Blacks in your circle about their anti-Blackness. And if you're ever approached with "How can I do better?" say nothing. But if you must say something, tell them they will need to go on that quest for themselves. Without you.

Racism is nothing new. Black people fighting for their civil rights is nothing new. If someone is just becoming aware of a system created to oppress nonwhites, then that's their problem. Not yours.

Say No

While there's nothing wrong with saying *yes* to things, it's more important to say *no*. Still, most of us find ourselves saying *yes* to things more than we say *no*. This is because we sometimes lack strong boundaries or have feelings of guilt around telling someone *no*. Think about the last time you said *yes* or *maybe* to something when you really wanted to say *no*. How did you feel? Resentful? Annoyed? Angry? Yeah, those aren't fun feelings.

When we don't honor our *no*, we are dishonoring *ourselves*. Saying *no* to things, like not picking up that extra shift because your manager asked, is a powerful thing. *No* has nothing to do with the other person you are telling it to. It has everything to do with you. When you tell others *no*, they must manage their own reaction to it. It is not our responsibility to make others feel comfortable with our *no*. We can say *no* and leave it at that.

You don't have to explain your *no* either. *No* is a full sentence. Need a push toward being more at ease with telling others *no*? Turn on "No Is Bae" by Toni Jones first thing in the morning and let the lyrics penetrate your mind. Being able to get comfortable with saying *no* is a power move for Black women. You take a stand against the societal expectation that you will take whatever is handed to you. Your life, your choice. Stand proud in your *no*. The biggest *yes* awaits you on your radical self-care journey.

Take a Break from Social Media

While social media can be used for good, it can also cause us to lose our sanity. Additionally, it can be a dangerous space for the mental wellness of Black women—and can also be loud.

Start your social media break by making the decision to commit to it. All you have to do is delete all the social media apps from your phone for a suitable allotted time. Suggested break time: at least two weeks. You will know you need to pause your use of social media when you realize you spend more time scrolling through your phone than being with the people in your own life.

Think about it. Social media is filled with people constantly sharing everything about themselves, from their thoughts to their daily meals. It breeds comparison and feeds impostor syndrome. You might engage in unhealthy magical thinking, which is creating beliefs that your thoughts or random events impact your future in a specific way. (*If I get a Brazilian Butt Lift, then my life will be better.*) It creates unnecessary pressure and can lead to increased experiences of anxiety, stress, and depression. Evaluate whether you are experiencing these negative emotions, then consider taking a hiatus from social media.

The benefits of taking a social media break are a clearer mind and an increased sense of self-worth. Your need to compare yourself to others will decrease. You will also begin to value what is in your world, distinguishing your daily life from your online presence.

Activate Your Anger

We create emotional distress for ourselves when we don't allow ourselves to activate specific emotions, like anger. Often, we limit our frustrations, afraid to be perceived as the "angry Black woman." This negative stereotype causes us to be perceived as hostile, ill-mannered, and overly aggressive when we display a normal emotion: anger. The real tea is that your fury intimidates others because of the strong influential power of Black women. Our anger is a threat because it creates historical movements and accomplishments.

Sis, when anger arises, sit in it without guilt, and channel it in a healthy direction. One of the most important ways to elevate your self-care is to tap into your emotions—something Black women are rarely given the opportunity to fully experience without pushing forward and ignoring our needs. This is no way to live.

Needless to say, anti-Blackness is at the root of the angry Black woman trope. However, it should not stop you from being angry. Your feelings are valid, and you have a right to be angry without others viewing you as a threat. White men get angry in the workplace and are patted on the back as others go above and beyond to calm their adult tantrum. White women get angry and weaponize their tears to harm others, especially Black women *and men*. Black women get angry, use their words skillfully to convey the reason behind their anger, and are deemed aggressive and needing to be handled in the same manner. *The audacity.* Give yourself permission to be unabashedly angry.

Validate Yourself after Experiencing Misogynoir

Misogynoir is one of the worst experiences a Black woman can encounter. Whenever you're unwarily mistreated, it can send you into a mental spiral of thoughts. *Did I get treated like this because I'm a woman? Were they rude or were they racist?* You begin to question your self-worth and actions, wondering what you did to deserve someone being racist and sexist toward you.

Truth is you did nothing to deserve that treatment. Nothing. People will dislike you and treat you ill simply because you are a Black woman. If you don't have access to someone you can process those hurtful feelings with, it's important to validate yourself. This means allowing yourself to believe what you experienced is true and all your emotions associated with that event are accurate. Following are some ways to validate yourself.

First, tell yourself some or all of the following statements: *I am allowed to feel this way. What happened to me, happened. I do not need to prove it to make it true. My perspective on things matters. Nothing is wrong with how I perceive things.* Next, write down what you experienced in a journal and revisit it another time or share it with a friend when you are ready. By validating your experience, you are validating your existence.

After giving yourself the gift of validation, you will feel better about yourself and your radical self-care efforts. There may be some lingering feelings of anger, but those negative emotions will not take up too much space in your brain.

Start Your Day with Silence

Starting your day with silence is a great way to kick-start your morning. If you're a parent, this can be a hard one. Silence and children don't go together. It will require you getting up earlier than usual. If you don't have kids, then praise be. Silence is easier for you to tap into.

Here are some suggested ways to start your day with silence. First, roll out of bed and head straight to the bathroom to start your morning routine. Next, make your way to the kitchen to make your coffee or tea, absorbing the aroma as it brews. Sit in silence as you finish your drink before doing anything else. Solitude is the best morning attitude, and quietness and stillness are how to begin your day with peace and ease. And sis, you need it. When you don't pick up your phone or turn on your TV and instead begin doing your morning rituals like nourishing your mind and your body, you are allowing yourself to listen to the most important person in your life: you. You can find clarity in the morning, so it's important to not be interrupted by noises that can distract your thoughts.

As you implement a quieter morning routine for yourself, you will have better days. Because before you face the world's judgment and nonsense of Black women, you need to be at peace with yourself. Find the time to listen to nothing but your inner self. Stillness is a goal you must achieve as you conquer radical self-care.

Identify Coping Skills

When it comes to your mental health, you are in charge. We can't control how others treat us, but we can control how we react. And when we find ourselves in stressful situations, it is important to identify coping skills so that we can de-escalate any feelings of anxiety or anger in the moment. Coping skills are tools, activities, or exercises, that help us manage our elevated emotions. They help us calm down. Figuring out what works for us as a Black woman may take time, and sometimes that one activity that worked in the past may not help us in the future. We have to constantly reevaluate what's going on and create an arsenal of emotional regulation tools that can help us manage unforeseen distress in a healthy way.

To identify coping skills, start by making notes of what helps you calm down when you experience little moments of anxiety or anger. A good coping skill is one that offers some distraction, moving our mind away from what's causing distress. It may or may not provide immediate relief, but it'll decrease any escalated feelings within minutes. Building self-awareness of how you react to and treat stress is how you create effective coping skills.

Ultimately, the self-soothing tools you use will help you manage the blows from microaggressions and other mistreatments you inevitably deal with as a Black woman. You will become less reactive to incidents of stress and more proactive about maintaining your mental wellness.

Follow Self-Help *Instagram* Accounts

Social media platforms like *Instagram* have allowed mental health professionals to share their expert knowledge with the world. And while *Instagram is not therapy*, it is a tool that can be used to enhance your self-care journey. You're already on your phone scrolling fifty-eleven times a day. Why not use your phone habit to benefit your emotional wellness?

There are several kinds of self-help *Instagram* accounts to follow. They include ones that provide mental health tips and resources, inspirational and relatable quotes, and images that bolster Black women. You will know you are following the right accounts when what is posted makes you feel better about yourself. Following culturally aligned self-help accounts will fill your mind with ways to empower your mental well-being. But beware; not all social media accounts are ours to follow. The mental health industry is influenced by research from white people, and the information shared by some clinicians can mimic these biases. It is important that you follow *Instagram* pages created to uplift Black women and that don't perpetuate a system that oppresses you.

Following self-help *Instagram* accounts allows us to see that we are not alone in whatever mental struggle we are facing. And thanks to the rise of self-help social media pages, access to mental health resources in the Black community has increased, and the stigma of mental health has decreased. So when you follow these accounts, you become part of an important wellness movement that encompasses your own radical self-care.

Watch a '90s Black TV Show

There's just something beneficial to the psyche about watching people who look like you act normal on a TV screen. Or your computer screen. Maybe even your smartphone. It signals to your mind that you, my dear, are a regular human being—despite how much society treats you like the other. So when you're feeling down or need a break from the world, go to your favorite streaming site and watch a '90s sitcom.

The '90s were poppin' for Black television. It was a different time. Shows were filmed in front of a live audience, and a variety of Black stories were told. *Black trauma, where?* We saw ourselves depicted in many ways. We were having fun with our friends on *Living Single*. Becoming adults in college on *A Different World*. Living bad and bougie on *The Fresh Prince of Bel-Air*. Showing off the power of Black love on *Martin*. Getting a regular science lesson on *Family Matters*. Embracing a different family structure on *Sister, Sister*. Acting a fool on *The Wayans Bros*. And appreciating so many more. Black television was powerful in the '90s. If you're not into the aforementioned shows, here are some others you might enjoy: *Hangin' with Mr. Cooper, Kenan & Kel, Moesha, The Hughleys, The Jamie Foxx Show, The Parent 'Hood,* and *The Steve Harvey Show*. Take your pick and use this time to celebrate the many faces of iconic Black television shows, some of which ultimately shaped our culture.

Stop Making Yourself Smaller

The hypervisibility that comes with being a Black woman can often make you feel like disappearing. Sometimes, you really do want to vanish into a wall to avoid people looking at you. You may find yourself trying to make yourself smaller in the rooms you step into. We do this because we want others to feel comfortable with our Blackness. One more thing that's not our responsibility.

Making yourself smaller is any action you take to diminish your presence. It can look like not speaking up in a group, sitting in the back away from people, censoring your true feelings when speaking, apologizing when it's unnecessary, and not sharing your accomplishments. We slowly teach ourselves through these actions that we do not matter, which fuels impostor syndrome and low self-esteem. The fact is, you matter, and you need to shine bright wherever you go.

To overcome this behavior, there will need to be some self-reflection and then action. When you begin to make yourself small in any situation, take note of it and reflect later about why. As you realize your why, commit to making one action to change this behavior—like speaking up at least once in your team meetings. Tiny steps to combating making your presence smaller will have a big reward. Enjoy them as you rediscover who you are on your radical self-care journey.

Ultimately, making yourself smaller doesn't feel good. The more you let go of doing this, the more self-assurance you will gain. The world is a better place when you believe in yourself.

Practice Accepting Compliments

A compliment is when someone tells you something nice about yourself without expectations. Sometimes it can be hard to accept compliments, especially for Black women. We often feel like we have to earn good praise. Think of the last time someone gave you a compliment. You probably reacted in one of these ways: You minimized the statement with a self-deprecating phrase, or you quickly deflected the attention elsewhere with a statement of comparison. *I don't think it looks that good on me. It would look better on you.* Most people who give compliments are not looking for anything in return. They just want you to know how fabulous you are and that you should recognize it as well.

Practice this exercise by reflecting on why it's so hard for you to accept compliments at times. Is it because you don't think you deserve receiving them? If so, why not? Next, practice simply saying "thank you" the next time you receive a compliment. Last, give compliments. This will build up your tolerance for being around them. You'll get into the groove of accepting compliments with this activity.

When you practice accepting compliments, you boost your self-esteem and mood. You begin to believe you are *that chick*, and you understand your road to radical self-care doesn't always have to be uncomfortable.

Ignore Race-Related News

Staying informed about what's going on in the world is fairly easy. We can consume news twenty-four hours a day, seven days a week if we want. However, constantly being exposed to race-related content is triggering, sis. It awakens strong emotions that stress our mind out.

Begin by creating measures to prevent your exposure to race-related news stories. Tap out of the news by scrolling past these kinds of stories on your social media newsfeed. Don't read that article. Don't even look at it. You can also ask friends to not share shocking news like this when they see it. And if you watch the news regularly, change the channel as soon as one of these stories comes on. However, if you want to stay informed but not traumatized, try glancing at a story without diving into the details. Consider turning off your TV after listening to the headlines.

The point is, we should not feed our mind with this stuff daily. Black trauma is not for mass consumption; it causes stress. It's time to ignore the fifty-eleventh article, post, or program of someone who looks like you being mistreated.

Ultimately, ignoring Black trauma news items will leave you in a better mood. This is a practice you can incorporate into your life how ever you see fit as you navigate your journey to radical self-care on your own terms. Hit these news stories with the swerve. It's for your mental wellness.

Have a Really Good Cry

Crying provides us with an emotional release. It's good for our mental health. However, activating our tears can sometimes be hard for a Black woman. To have a really good cry, simply turn on a sad movie and let the tears fall without judgment. Snot bubbles and all. Cry in private for inner peace.

Never underestimate the power of a good cry. Not one that requires only a couple dabs with a tissue on the side of your eyes. An ugly cry that involves wailing. Your nose is stuffed up afterward. Your eyes are bloodshot. Your chest is pounding from all the heaving you've done. Your cheeks are soft and damp.

Most of the time, Black women are expected to hold on to our sad, stressful emotions. Additionally, the messages we received as children told us to cry less and laugh more—even when feeling sad. Think about how many times you were told to not cry while you were crying as a kid. If no one has told you yet, *it is okay to cry.*

Life gets stressful, and crying has been found to help get rid of that stress. It is one of the quickest ways to activate feel-good chemicals like endorphins that are living inside us. You will instantly boost your mood after you let the tears fall. You will heal your emotional pain, which is vital to your radical self-care. Afterward, you will be lightheaded for two reasons: the excessive crying and the emotional release.

Limit Interactions with Well-Meaning White People

One thing that is worse than overtly racist white people is well-meaning white people. The difference between the two groups is that the latter doesn't think they are racist. (*whispers* *They are.*) Well-meaning white people are individuals who are usually the perpetrators of microaggressions. These wypipo request our assistance in being better allies by burdening us with questions about race. These whytes go out of their way to try to portray that they are not racist by telling us things like *I don't see color. I would've voted for Obama for a third term if I could.* Sure, Jan.

Well-meaning white folks seemingly want to dismantle white supremacy but are also happy to reap its societal benefits. We're still perceived as the other by them. Interacting with these people does damage to our emotional health. We could develop something called *white people fatigue* if left unchecked. It's where you're so tired of dealing with white people and their shenanigans that you avoid them at all costs. This means walking around with resentment. That negative emotion is not ours to carry. Get ahead of it and simply limit your interactions with well-meaning white people.

Some ways to limit your interactions: Walk away from conversations about race between white people. Ignore direct messages from childhood white friends you haven't talked to in decades who ask, *How are you?* It's a trap. They just want to make sure they weren't one of the racist wypipo in your life. Limit your interactions so you can take care of yourself.

As you practice this exercise, you will instantly feel better because you are preventing emotional fatigue and deterioration you no longer need to carry on your discovery of radical self-care.

Write Out Affirmations

Affirmations are one of the best ways to take control over our mental health. If you're not familiar with them, they are statements that clear our thoughts and increase positive thinking. These statements are powerful. And as a Black woman, we need all the empowerment we can get to counteract the negative messages we receive about our existence from society.

One way to ensure that you are consuming affirmations is to write them down on a sticky notepad and place them around your home. Consider writing this one down: *I am breaking generational curses by healing myself.* This is a powerful statement, because as a Black woman, your healing results in the freedom of the women in the generations that follow. Read it and repeat it to yourself throughout the day, and you will begin to see your thoughts and behaviors change for the better.

As you use affirmations to improve your mental wellness, you will activate your motivation for personal growth. You will be able to regulate your emotions and experience the freedom that comes along with increased self-confidence as you continue to navigate your radical self-care journey. Affirmations not only change the way we think, but they can literally change our lives. They help us create beliefs that encourage us to be the best version of ourselves. The more we say affirmations, the more we believe them. The more we believe them, the better we feel.

Don't Become Someone's Emotional Dumping Ground

Exploitation of Black women's labor is the world's favorite pastime. Be cautious of those seeking to take advantage of you, sis. They are everywhere. Many will attempt to suck you dry of your knowledge, your time, and your skills. Especially when they are in distress.

If you are naturally a very nurturing person, those in need of care will find their way to you. Put a stop to it soon as you see it heading your way. Otherwise, you will be used as an emotional rehabilitation center. Your emotional wellness tank will be drained of every last empathy drop. There will be none for you to give to yourself when you need it most.

Because Black women are the best supporters, people often feel comfortable using us as a dumping ground for their emotions. However, you don't have space for everybody to be telling you their business.

What to say to people when they begin to unload their emotional distress on you:

- "Sorry. I don't have the emotional capacity right now to handle any stress you are going through."
- "I don't have the space to deal with this right now. I will let you know when I can talk."
- "Sounds like you are going through a lot. I don't have the time to sit and listen to you right now."

Your peace is your responsibility; how others react is not. You will feel relieved after declining to carry someone else's bags instead of your own as you manage your mental health.

Use Guided Meditations

Meditation sounds more intimidating than it is. You're probably thinking, *That ain't for me. My mind is always racing.* Well, if you wanna decrease your experience with emotional distress, you need to give meditating a try—especially as you prioritize self-care.

Meditation is top-tier when it comes to taking care of our mental health. It's the practice of focusing or monitoring our thoughts for a time. When we meditate, we calm our mind, improve our attention, and reconnect to ourselves. We regulate emotions and learn to self-soothe. By introducing meditation to your self-care practice, you are creating an exclusively safe space to release emotions. You are training your mind to be aware of all that is in and around you.

Meditation doesn't always have to look like sitting down for twenty minutes and trying to swat away stressful thoughts. Even if you're a beginner, you can use guided meditations. It feels less overwhelming when you have someone else leading you.

To find the right guided meditations, start by searching *YouTube* for what fits your needs, like the length and topic. If that doesn't work, consider downloading apps that fit the style of meditation you want. Some app suggestions include Headspace: Meditation & Sleep, Liberate: Black Meditation App, and Shine: Calm Anxiety & Stress.

Meditation helps clear the mind. Something we desperately need as we deal with symptoms of race-based traumatic stress. As we calm our minds, we improve our mental wellness. You'll feel happy, relaxed, and peaceful when you practice daily meditations as part of your radical self-care.

Listen to a Podcast

The last decade has seen a surge in the creation of podcasts. There's just something enjoyable about listening to episodes of people talking about a specific topic, especially as it relates to you as a Black woman. Thanks to the Internet, just about anyone can create a podcast on anything. And thank goodness. The world needs a variety of voices pushing out content.

One way to enjoy a podcast is to listen to it while you're driving to work or going on a walk. It's the kind of self-care we deserve. Let your mind rest, tune out the world, and get lost in whatever is being shared into your ears.

No matter what kind of podcast you're into, there is something for you. However, to optimize this activity, consider listening to empowering conversations from women who look like (and probably sound like) you. Here are some podcasts to consider adding to your playlist: *Brown Girl Self-Care*; *Jill Scott Presents: J.ill the Podcast*; *Okay, Now Listen*; *Ratchet & Respectable*; *Small Doses with Amanda Seales*; and *Therapy for Black Girls*. And as you indulge in a podcast by some sistahs on your road to radical self-care, you'll get to let your mind unwind and relax. No stress, just good vibes and entertainment.

Stop Watching Black Trauma Entertainment

Just like tuning out race-related news, not watching Black trauma entertainment should rank high on your to-do self-care list. Hollywood *loves* creating shows and films about Black people that are rooted in our historical trauma. Why? Because it sells. Our real pain is often meant for non-Black people to enjoy as they watch from behind a screen. The caucasity.

Entertainment that centers Black pain like police brutality, sexual assault against Black women, racism in all of its forms, slavery, the civil rights movement, etc. can feel like important stories to be told. And while some are, most are not. It's sickening for the mind, as a Black person, to be triggered emotionally as you watch a movie. Why put yourself through two hours of that? It's like inflicting pain on yourself. That's why it's a strong no for me, dawg. Watching these shows and movies only fuels the fire in directors and producers to create more Black trauma. If they see the success of these pieces, they will feel inclined to create more. It's dehumanizing and only perpetuates the stereotype of Black people being perceived in one way. So save your mind the drama and skip the Black trauma. Actively choose to only watch entertainment that involves Black normalcy and joy for a smoother radical self-care experience.

Simplify Your Goals

When it comes to achieving goals, it's better to simplify. To do this, create an objective for what you're trying to accomplish. An objective is a realistic action you can take. For example: Your goal is to meditate for twenty minutes, but you've never meditated before. Your objective is to try daily meditations for one minute, adding an extra minute each day until you get to twenty.

Setting goals in small attainable steps makes the impossible seem possible. The idea of simplifying them is to create tiny movements that get us up the mountain. We'll resist the need to overwork or burn out to reach our achievements. Sooner than later, we'll be at the top looking back at our progress. Get started creating the goals you need to attain the life you've been waiting for.

Sometimes, having big dreams can be overwhelming. We can get consumed by our doubt and fear of the road ahead. We begin to have negative thoughts like *How will I ever do that? Should I even try? I might as well give up.* It's especially hard for Black women, because we are often the trailblazer in our bloodline, venturing out and attempting to reach a goal no one in our family has accomplished. And when our mind is overloaded with negative emotions, it gets clouded, causing us to lose our motivation. Creating a simple plan to actually follow helps establish a clear guide to your radical self-care goals.

Focus On the Present Workday

If you're like many people, then you probably don't like your job. If nobody told you, it's okay to not like your job, even if you enjoy the kind of work you do. You may even have your dream job, and it can still be a pain in your butt.

Sometimes, a job is simply a way for us to collect a paycheck for the skills we have. That is perfectly fine, as long as we're keeping those boundaries at work and focusing on other things that bring us joy. However, it can be hard to feel motivated to work a job we don't particularly enjoy. Here's why it's important to practice focusing on your current workday. When you're feeling exploited at your job, because that's what workplaces like to do to Black women, take it one day at a time.

To do this, try the following: When Monday comes around, don't focus on how far away Friday is. (*I know. It's so freaking far.*) Instead, shift your attention to your tasks for the day. Tell yourself, *I just gotta get to the end of the workday, and then the rest of the day is mine.*

Allowing ourselves to stay present and focused on the current workday is a mindfulness act that will help decrease any anxiety we may have about the workweek. Fear of the anticipated week—a.k.a. the Sunday scaries—will go away as you focus your intentions only on present-day radical self-care methods.

Rewatch Your Favorite Movie or TV Show

Is there a movie or television series you've watched at least five times, and you haven't gotten sick of it yet? Who wants to watch *Girlfriends* again? Anyone?

Watching something we are very familiar with is good for our emotional wellness. When we sit back, relax, and indulge in a film or TV show that we can basically recollect scene for scene and quote word for word, we're easing any feelings of anxiety. What causes most anxiety is fear of the unknown. There's just something about knowing what's coming next that calms us down. We don't have to worry about being surprised by any violence or sadness. We already know the emotions that will be evoked. And if it's a movie or show we've seen for the fifty-eleventh time, we're already emotionally prepared.

There are many ways to do this exercise. One of the best times to watch your favorite movie is right after work. It's the perfect way to unwind after a really long day. You can also treat yourself to a weekend binge of your favorite TV show. Silence your phone and stream that show of yours. No judgment if you never change out of your sleepwear. And as you get lost in your favorite scenes, you will feel calmer. Any current feelings of stress or anxiety because of microaggressions you recently experienced will be released. Total relaxation will be activated, and you will be grateful you had this time to yourself to unwind on your radical self-care journey.

Part 2
BODY

Taking care of our physical health is vital to our well-being. Sometimes, negative emotions get trapped in our bodies and need to be released. When feelings like anger, fear, or doubt do not exit our system, they can fester into physical ailments. Muscle aches become our best friend. Joints join the stubborn pain club. Sicknesses place a hold on our schedules. You must take action by practicing self-care for your body.

In this section, you will discover exercises and activities that require you to become an active participant in your pursuit of radical self-care. You will be encouraged to get up and move while being gentle with and attentive to the needs of your body. You'll feel empowered to make your body a safer space for you. Your home.

Participate in a Protest

As Black women, we do not have the privilege of ignoring political issues. Our very existence is considered an act of protest. Our brown skin and kinky hair fight against Eurocentric beauty standards. Our academic achievements help dismantle the racial disparities in the education system. Our occupational goals assist in closing the wage gap. The inequities that exist in society impact us on an individual and institutional level. And when it comes to social injustice issues we care about, we can feel like we do not have a voice. The system at large has made it harder for us to witness and experience change. We feel stifled. Stuck. Hopeless. Well, no more. It's time to take back your power by participating in a protest for your radical self-care.

Start by finding a grassroots or local organization that is tackling a problem you care about. These groups always have an action plan. You can locate an organization in your neighborhood by searching online, visiting your community center, or looking through your newspapers or magazines. This is a great place to be active about issues close to your heart while meeting new people and influencing change. What starts local can become global.

Ultimately, gathering in the streets with people who share your interest in an important cause is invigorating for your body. Every part of your being will come alive as you get involved in a political movement. You will feel empowered as you pound the pavement chanting things like *No justice! No peace!* Get involved.

Find a Black Doctor

Finding the right healthcare provider is key to maintaining our physical well-being. And for Black women, it can literally be a matter of life and death because implicit bias impacts how doctors treat us in a medical setting. Our needs are routinely ignored by our care team. It has been reported that many doctors believe we are lying about our pain levels, or they think we can withstand more. The result of this discriminatory treatment is misdiagnosing, prolonging diseases or illnesses, and for many Black women, death. It's no surprise that the mortality rate from pregnancy is three times higher for Black mothers than white mothers. Black women are routinely ignored or dismissed by healthcare providers. Which is why we need to find a Black doctor who will be attentive to our needs and listen to our concerns.

Begin your search with your health insurance. Most providers will allow you to search by medical field and gender. Put finding a Black primary care doctor and gynecologist at the top of your search. Consider also using online databases like BlackDoctor.org, Health in Her HUE, and the Association of Black Women Physicians. Shop around before committing to a doctor. You want to make sure you've chosen the right healthcare provider.

All in all, having a doctor who looks like you will ease any feelings of anxiety you may have about the medical system. You will be able to feel assured that you have a healthcare provider who can see your humanity and give you the adequate treatment you deserve.

Tap Deeper Into Your Femininity

Our femininity is our superpower. It's our secret sauce. Feminine energy requires us to be things like vulnerable, empathetic, and receptive. We get to intuitively operate in our senses, being gentle to ourselves and others. Black women are often placed in a position that demands us to be the exact opposite. We are asked to put out masculine energy. We are forced to be things like assertive, strong, and giving. We have to move from a place of logic to protect ourselves and others. Both energies are different and serve their purpose. Neither is associated with gender.

However, if we're always living in a state of masculinity, we never get to experience the freedom of femininity. Tapping deeper into your feminine energy will enhance the way you feel about yourself.

To awaken your femininity, find an activity that makes you feel free and adorned. Perhaps it's taking a day off to do whatever you want without a set schedule. Or, maybe it's sparking spontaneity by taking an unplanned day trip. You can also try expressing yourself through a creative outlet like dancing, cooking, singing, or painting—or putting on your favorite outfit just because you feel and look good in it. Lastly, you can arouse any of your five senses by taking time out to do something for yourself like dry brushing your body or smelling your favorite essential oils. Play around and discover what works for you.

The goal of getting better in touch with your femininity is to feel more balanced in your body. What's great about doing an exercise that releases your feminine energy is that you will feel more confident and replenished. The way you approach people and situations will be different. A softer, more relaxed, and clearer-headed version of you will be present everywhere you go on your newfound journey of radical self-care.

Oil Your Scalp

When it comes to taking care of our hair, our curly strands are not the only part of our crown that needs love. Our scalp does too. Yes, we need to moisturize our tresses, but providing our scalp with some specialized care will improve the quality of our hair too. It is important for Black women to regularly oil our scalp because it tends to get drier quicker than other hair textures. While our kinky coils suck up all the moisture, our scalp becomes parched. Therefore, we need to create time to properly care for our hair.

Start by finding an oil of your choice. Perhaps it's a natural oil like castor oil, or it's a product that is specifically formulated to treat something like dandruff. Either way, explore and discover what works for you. Aside from wash day, the best time to oil your scalp is right before bed. So, grab your oil. Now, part your hair into sections and go through each area with your fingers or a rat tail comb. Next, apply the oil to your scalp as you see fit, massaging it into your head and throughout your hair. Repeat until finished. You should aim to do this every day.

After you oil your scalp, you'll feel relaxed. Slowing down and carving out time for you to nurture your crown will not only be beneficial to your hair, but it'll make you feel good about yourself as you figure out how to get things done on your road to radical self-care. You're taking care of you.

Create Art

In a world where we are constantly being told what we should or shouldn't do as a Black woman, creating art is a great way to regain a sense of autonomy. Art is one of the magical wonders of the world. It is subjective. What one person likes, another may not. Yet, it can bring people together. And while engaging in art is a unique experience for every person, it is also beneficial to our health. Research has found that making art for forty-five minutes can reduce the level of cortisol (a.k.a. stress hormone) coursing through our bodies. Thus, we've gotta incorporate art into our radical self-care routine.

Get into creating art by playing around with what interests you. Art comes in so many forms. Start by finding a class for drawing, painting, or sculpting. Purchase an adult coloring book (yes, those exist) and explore colored pencils, crayons, markers, etc. Explore your photography skills by using a digital camera or your phone to take pictures. Your artistic choices are endless. Begin with something small and see where it takes you.

Overall, participating in some type of artistic activity lowers your stress and anxiety. You feel more relaxed, and your mood improves. The best part is that creating art helps you have a better understanding of yourself. Through the art-making process, you learn to free yourself from any mental or physical constraints holding you back. You also build self-confidence by taking control of the kind of art you make. Now, that's what's up.

Stretch Before Bed

Getting a good night's rest is essential for maintaining our physical health. It allows our body to recover from long, hard days of dealing with everyday stressors. Like fighting off the stings of microaggressions. By the time we get home, we're exhausted. And when it's time to go to bed, sometimes it can be hard to calm down our body. The effects of our daily life can cause stress, anxiety, and even depression. This can keep us up at night.

To combat your inability to fall asleep, try stretching before bed. Stretching activates your parasympathetic nervous system (PNS). Your PNS is responsible for your body's rest and digestion functionality. Its main priority is to restore and rebuild your body, and it is activated when you are in a state of relaxation.

One stretch guaranteed to make you feel relaxed instantly is a yoga pose called Standing Forward Bend, a.k.a. *Uttanasana*. Start by standing with your feet together. Inhale and exhale. Bend forward from your hips, not your waist. Focus on lengthening your torso and letting your head hang. Go as far down as you can. Attempt to touch the floor. Modify by bending your knees, standing with your legs apart, or holding on to a chair. Hold for thirty seconds. Come out of the pose by gently rising and keeping your spine straight.

After you complete a stretch like the previous suggestion, you will feel calm and relieved of any distress. Don't be surprised if afterward you fall asleep almost immediately as you embrace radical self-care.

Go on a Long Walk

Taking a long walk is therapeutic. It is not only good for our body; it is also good for our mind and spirit. When we make space to take a walk for an extended period, we're choosing ourselves. We're selecting to improve our physical fitness, as well as find internal peace. Walking is a low-pressure form of exercise; we can walk as fast or as slow as we want and still achieve a great workout. There is power in walking. With each step, we heal the pain that comes with the experience of being a Black woman. With each stride, we harness the strength that lives within us to make a difference in our community. Hence, adding a long walk to your self-care toolbox is a must.

Begin your journey by deciding what you will listen to on your walk. Select your favorite album or playlist. Or choose an episode of a podcast you like or an audiobook. Decide your route and estimate your time. The best long walks are at least an hour. Be safe and go when the sun is out, making sure you're back home before sunset. Consider picking a destination with a purpose. Like walking to the store to buy a bottle of water or a snack.

After a long walk, you will be euphoric. You will feel accomplished and have an elevated mood because of the endorphins released from your physical and radical self-care journey. The day's worries will be left outside where you strolled on without them.

Cook Your Favorite Meal

Cooking is the perfect addition to our self-care routine. So, put away the McDonald's money and step into the kitchen. Start by looking up the recipe for your favorite meal. Make sure you have all the ingredients on hand. If not, take a trip to the grocery store for your necessities. Grab the kitchenware you'll need: pots, pans, cutting boards, knives, spoons, measuring utensils, etc. Turn on some music and begin to cook. Follow or stray from the recipe of choice as much as you like. Get lost in the sauce and enjoy the process of cooking.

After you're done preparing your favorite meal, you will feel calm. The stress that was living in your body no longer resides within. And focusing on what you were cooking allowed your mind to enter a meditative state and forget your anxieties for radical self-care. You will also feel accomplished because you get to enjoy the final product: a dish you made.

When society drains us of all our energy, and we're tired of things like being the spokesperson for Black people in our environment, cooking provides us with the space to decompress. Preparing a meal is not just an activity we regularly do to nourish our body. It's how we effectively combat stress. The benefits of cooking include releasing body tension, boosting mood, sharpening brain skills, increasing self-confidence, igniting creativity, and nourishing our bodies with good food. And the best way to enhance these benefits? Cook something you love. *Bon appétit!*

Take a Bubble Bath

There's taking a bath, and then there's taking a bubble bath. Similar activities, but the latter sparks a little more joy. Think of the last time you took a bubble bath. It's probably been a long time. So, take this as your sign to treat yourself to one immediately. Soaking in the tub with bubbles has a ton of health benefits. You'll relieve muscle pain, body aches, and skin conditions. You'll also elevate your mood, improve your quality of sleep, and boost your immune system. *Wow.* And after a week of having to work twice as hard as your white counterparts at work or school, you deserve one.

Start by turning on music or lighting candles. Next, draw yourself a bath before bedtime. Pour in your soap of choice, but avoid pouring too much or you'll have an overflow of bubbles. If you want, add Epsom salt to help with pain relief or your favorite bath bomb with essential oils for aromatherapy. Turn on the water, making sure it's not too hot. Fill up the bathtub halfway and gently slide in. Cleanse yourself and then soak up the suds for ten to fifteen minutes. Read a book, play with the bubbles, or simply do nothing. Once you're finished, dry yourself and moisturize. Drain the tub and head to bed for the best sleep of your life.

Ultimately, a bubble bath is a self-care necessity. Afterward, any stress, anxiety, or feelings of depression you were carrying will wash away. You'll emerge from the bath with a clearer head and more relaxed body.

Wear Your Natural Hair

As a Black woman, we've been made to feel that our natural hair is not beautiful. The messaging starts at a young age. We are tricked into believing straight hair is "good hair." So, we agree to the stings and burns of a chemical relaxer. This teaches us to ignore our pain and to hide our identity. And as we grow up, society doubles down on this message. We are denied jobs because our natural hair is seen as unprofessional. We are singled out at school because our kinky coils are seen as unkempt. Our natural hair is weaponized and politicized when all we want is to exist as our authentic selves. Consequently, many resort to tucking our hair under different weaves. But there's no need to hide your gorgeous curls anymore. If you haven't already, consider starting your natural hair journey at once.

Begin however you see fit: Do the big chop; cut off all your hair. Or, transition by stretching out your new growth to a length you like, and cut off your relaxed hair. If you choose to transition instead of chop, do not apply heat to your hair, and wear low-manipulation or protective styles like wigs and braids. After you transition to natural hair, another level of radical self-care discovery begins.

Going natural will be exciting. Aside from saving money on salon trips, you will get to explore your natural hair—learning what styles and products work best for you. Most importantly, you will gain self-acceptance, shedding the belief that your hair is not beautiful.

Reclaim Ownership over Your Body

Sometimes, as a Black woman, we can feel like our body is not ours. The training to relinquish ownership of our body is generational. Historically, the Black female body has always been subjected to objectification (example: the story of Sarah Baartman). But for us, it begins in childhood.

Black girls are often seen as more mature; thus we are sexualized at an early age. We are taught that our body exists for the display or pleasure of others and not our own. Needless to say, the sexualization of Black women carries into adulthood. Men, media, and others obsess over everything about us. From our shape to the shade of our skin, nothing is free from objectification. Pressure is put on us to have a more curvaceous body because Black women are stereotyped for having a bootylicious figure. Criticism follows us for how light or dark our skin appears, with one shade being deemed prettier than the other. The messages we receive from society are exhausting to absorb. It turns our bodies into a place we cannot call home, because we are uncomfortable in our skin. But enough is enough. You need to reclaim ownership over your body.

Take back dominion over your body by first embracing the way you were created. Look in the mirror and tell yourself you are beautiful. Realize that every perceived physical imperfection was designed perfectly for you. Next, make decisions about your body that are solely influenced by you. Only put things (or people) in, on, or around your body that honor and respect you. Lastly, stop comparing yourself to other women. No two bodies need to look the same. These are ongoing activities you must practice with intention.

As a result, your self-esteem will increase. Any obsessive thoughts about the way your body looks will wither away. You will feel empowered and fall in love with yourself every day. This is a good thing as it relates to your latest radical self care endeavors.

Find an Enjoyable Exercise

It is well known that exercising is an important component to maintaining a healthy body. The benefits of working out include improved mood, weight management, increased energy, and most importantly, sickness and disease prevention. And when it comes to health conditions that specifically kill Black women more than any other race, preventable diseases like heart disease, stroke, diabetes, and hypertension rank high on that list.

To find an exercise you like, start by getting involved in some group workouts. Join a gym with fitness classes. Check out your local community center—like a YMCA—and try out the workout classes offered. Lastly, you can also snag a free trial of ClassPass, an app that allows you to try different kinds of fitness classes. Explore what interests you. And when you locate a workout that feels like a fun challenge, you've found the one.

Ultimately, engaging in a fitness activity you truly enjoy will keep you motivated to continue working out. The more you exercise, the better you feel about yourself. Because as you actively improve your physical wellness, you will be increasing your self-confidence. You learn to love your body. You become more focused. But most significantly, you prevent yourself from becoming another mortality statistic and get to continue your radical self-care healing. Our life expectancy literally depends on us moving our body. Feeling motivated to work out can be hard. Still, you must find an exercise you enjoy. If you love the activity, you'll continue to do it.

Take a Nap

Rest is essential to taking care of our body. Yet, the world may try to tell us otherwise. Environments like our workplace and school ask us to buy into the "team no sleep" culture. They make attempts to convince us that there are wins from burning out. We get inundated with unrealistic workloads and little to no rewards because people seem to think Black women have a higher capacity for hard labor. However, there's nothing cute about being sleep-deprived. When we're not getting enough rest, our body doesn't function well. We become irritable. We can't focus. We complete tasks inaccurately. We crave unhealthy snacks to fight off fatigue. Does this sound like you? Then you need to take a nap.

Prepare for your nap by setting an alarm clock. Decide how long you need to sleep in the afternoon. If you want to take a short nap, then set your alarm for ten or twenty minutes. But if you want to take a longer one, because you're running on an empty sleep tank, set your alarm for ninety minutes or two hours. Grab your bonnet and enjoy your nap. You deserve it.

After your short beauty rest, you should feel refreshed and energized to take on what's left of your day as you realign your physical wellness with your radical self care goals.

Advocate for Your Health

The healthcare system is not nice to Black women. Historically, Black women have been abused by the medical field. In the nineteenth century, enslaved Black women were experimented on without anesthesia for the sake of women's reproductive health research. And in current times, Black women's physical needs are consistently ignored by doctors. You can probably think of a time when you mentioned a health issue to a doctor and they simply dismissed your concern. This then led to either a bigger health problem or years of you going untreated for a specific diagnosis. It's discouraging. You feel silenced and abandoned, not knowing which medical professionals to trust. Well, it's time to relinquish the feeling that you are powerless. It's time to use your voice and advocate for your health.

To speak up about your health concerns, let go of the feeling that your doctor knows more about your body than you because they are the medical professional. You live in your own body. You know it best. You know when something just doesn't feel right. Tell your doctor about all your ailments. Provide any research you have done on your health concern. If the doctor provides you with an unsatisfactory answer, go and get a second opinion. Find a medical professional who will provide you with adequate care.

When you advocate for your health, you will feel empowered. This is a welcome change as you continue your radical self-care. Yes, it will be frustrating at first, but your health matters. Speak up for your needs and don't back down without being heard.

Customize Your Supplement Plan

Our bodies require certain nutrients to thrive. This includes vitamins and minerals to protect our organs and prevent chronic illnesses. Most of the recommended essential elements that help us maintain a healthy body can be found in food. But depending on our diet and age, we may be missing out on key nutrients. In comes the need for supplements. Research finds that many Black women tend to be deficient in the following vitamins and minerals: calcium, iron, magnesium, and vitamin D—to name a few. Thus, to make sure you're keeping your body in tip-top shape, create a customized supplement plan.

Before you update your supplement regimen, consult with your physician or medical provider. Get blood work done to see what vitamins and minerals you are lacking. It's important to know what's going on in your body before you start taking any kind of supplement. Ingesting an excessively high amount of nutrients can be just as detrimental to your health as being deficient. Once you're aware of what vitamins and minerals your body needs, decide how you will consume them. Supplements come in many forms, such as, pills, gummies, liquids, and powders. Find what works best for you.

Ultimately, establishing a supplement routine for yourself will give you a sense of control over your physical well-being. You'll feel empowered to continue engaging in practices that improve your health in the direction you're moving in on your radical self-care journey. Your body will thank you.

Drink More Water

Want to improve your quality of life? Stay hydrated...*and mind your business*. It's no secret that water is one of the key elements to maintaining a healthy body. With most of our body being made up of water, all our organs need it to function. Our body uses water to do things like absorb nutrients, lubricate joints, and flush out toxins. Go without water and you'll experience dehydration, which can cause a foggy brain, heat exhaustion, and poor bowel movements. Additionally, studies have found that Black women tend to drink less water when compared to other races. Therefore, you need to start consuming more water today.

Begin by figuring out how much water you must drink every day. It's recommended that we consume half our weight in ounces. For example, if you weigh two hundred pounds, then you should try to consume one hundred ounces of water each day. Next, get motivated to drink more water by trying one of these techniques: Carry a water bottle around, switch up your intake with herbal teas, infuse your water with lemon and other fruits, or eat more fruits and vegetables. Be sure to pace yourself, drinking half your daily water intake by the afternoon. Follow these suggestions and you'll be well hydrated.

The results of drinking more water may include more trips to the bathroom to urinate, but your skin will glow, your mind will be clear, and your body will be happy and healthy. Radical self-care starts with a healthy dose of H_2O. Pour yourself a glass and enjoy it.

Spend Time in the Sun

Feeling stressed? Go outside and bask in the sun. Exposing ourselves to the sun is not only critical for our health, it's also the quickest way to boost our mood. When the sun hits the melanin in our skin, it's not just making us feel warm and happy. The sun activates the cells in our bodies to do what they do best: Take care of us. You see, our body naturally increases the production of vitamin D in response to our skin's exposure to sunlight. Vitamin D plays a major role in the way our body's immunity works, doing things like regulating the amount of calcium in our body, which is needed to maintain healthy bones, teeth, and muscles. And unfortunately, Black women tend to lack a sufficient amount of vitamin D in our system. Thus, regularly spending time in the sun should be added to your self-care routine as soon as possible.

To work sunbathing into your life, start by spending ten to thirty minutes a day in the sun. Find opportunities to briefly get some sunlight, like eating your lunch outside. Just make sure you don't burn your skin with overexposure. Wear sunscreen and stay hydrated. Your body will love you for doing this.

All in all, getting some daily sunlight is beneficial for your body. You will have better moods, feeling calmer and more focused throughout the day. In addition, you will notice an improved sleep cycle, which will further promote radical self-care. But most importantly, your body will feel rejuvenated and pampered.

Eat More Plants

Our gut is like our second brain. What we eat impacts how we think, feel, and behave. Ever feel sluggish after having a really big, greasy meal? There's a reason for that. Studies report there is something called the gut-brain axis. This is the communication pathway between our brain and stomach. These two parts of our body are constantly talking back and forth to each other through our gut microbiota, which is a collection of microorganisms like bacteria and fungi. The more diverse the microbiota is in our stomach, the better it is for our health. Plant foods like fruits, vegetables, nuts, and grains contain fiber, which increases the different kinds of good bacteria and fungi in our gut. If we have better gut microbiota, positive hormones and other messages will be sent up to our brain, influencing our emotional and physical well-being. And because the reality is that more Black women are dying from preventable diseases, switching up our diet is a great start to combating these deadly diagnoses.

First off, you don't need to go full-on vegan or vegetarian to begin reaping the benefits of eating more plants. Simply commit to adding more plant-based foods to everyday meals. Begin with eating more of your favorite fruits, vegetables, nuts, and grains. For example, if you love mangoes (*who doesn't?!*), figure out a way to eat more. Cut one up and have it with your breakfast or toss it in a smoothie. Then, consider looking up recipes that involve mangoes and get creative in the kitchen. Additionally, make sure you're consuming pre-biotics and probiotics. Probiotic foods like yogurt are good bacteria. Prebiotic foods like oatmeal feed the friendly bacteria. The more frequently you eat plants, the more your taste buds will crave foods that are good for your gut.

Overall, eating more plants is beneficial for your physical and mental health. As you embrace a healthier diet, you will have more energy, possibly drop a few pounds, and feel good about yourself. The road to radical self-care is full of gut-healthy options; give it a try.

Set an Alarm for Bed

Getting a good night's rest is how we maintain a healthy body. More importantly, being consistent in the number of hours we sleep every night is crucial. However, this can be difficult because as a Black woman, you may have adopted a warped view of rest already. With constantly having to prove the importance of our existence in oppressive environments, we become conditioned to seeing rest as something that must be earned. You might find yourself engaging in sleep-sabotaging behavior, such as finishing up last-minute work assignments or aimlessly scrolling on social media. Either way, you need a plan to protect your ability to get enough sleep at night. Hence, setting an alarm for when it's time to go to bed is exactly what you need to do. Creating this reminder will help you be consistent with your sleep cycle *if you utilize it.*

First, figure out what time you would like to go to sleep and wake up. Set your alarm to go to bed at least an hour before your desired sleep time. These sixty minutes before your bedtime will be your wind-down hour. It's where you will engage in any rituals that help you fall asleep. This hour also gives you ample time to ditch any sleep-sabotaging activities. *cough* *Put your phone away.* *cough*

A well-managed sleep routine will have you feeling more grounded and prepared for your next day of radical self-care.

Pay Attention to Your Periods

It's time for a flow check—if you have one. How are your periods? Are they long or short? Heavy or light? Painful or painless? Irregular or regular? The behavior of our monthly flow indicates what's going on in our body. That's why it's important to pay attention to our periods, especially as a Black woman. Do you know Black women are more likely to go years (sometimes, decades) undiagnosed and untreated for conditions like endometriosis and polycystic ovary syndrome? Another implication of how Black women receive treatment—or lack thereof. Many sistahs suffer from period problems, and nothing is done about it until the issue reaches a boiling point. Your flow issues get dismissed and you're misdiagnosed or mistreated. But when it comes to medical conditions related to your ovaries and uterus, the earlier the treatment, the better. So, start paying attention to your periods and take action.

Foremost, track your periods. Use a flow tracking app or a calendar. If you're not getting your period on a monthly basis, and you're not experiencing extra stress or on any form of birth control like an IUD, speak to your doctor. Additionally, if your flow is excruciatingly painful or very heavy for more than ten days, seek medical treatment.

Ultimately, you don't need to suffer in silence from period problems. Be aware of what's going on down there with your flow and advocate for treatment if things don't feel right. A better monthly period experience and a better radical self-care opportunity await you.

Wear Sunscreen

While that gorgeous brown skin of ours glistens in the sun, we need to make sure we protect it from the sun's rays. Begin by incorporating sunscreen into your everyday life. Purchase a facial moisturizer with at least an SPF of 30. Additionally, cover your body in your favorite sunscreen. Find one that doesn't leave a white residue, like the brand Black Girl Sunscreen. Just because we've got lots of melanin in our skin doesn't mean it can't get burned. So, we need to wear sunscreen.

In addition to protecting our skin from getting sunburned, sunscreen prevents us from developing skin cancer. It's a myth that Black folks don't need to wear sun protectant cream. While we may not burn easily or catch skin cancer as often as our white counterparts, it still happens. Black people simply tend to get diagnosed with skin cancer at a later stage because many do not wear sunscreen nor do regular skin checks for cancerous moles. Don't be like this, sis. Put on the sunscreen. And protect your skin further by being proactive.

Make a yearly dermatology appointment to have your body checked for any possibly problematic moles. In the long run, wearing sunscreen on a daily basis will provide your melanin-rich skin with the extra protection it needs on your radical self-care journey. You'll be keeping your body healthy by preventing skin cancer and other consequences of sun damage.

Order Takeout

Give yourself a night off in the kitchen and order takeout. A home-cooked meal is great, but sometimes, we just need to have a meal that isn't immediately followed by washing dishes. Think of it as a treat for yourself. We deserve an evening of not hovering over a stove as we put a meal together. And although takeout is a wonderful way to reward yourself, remember that Black women tend to suffer more from preventable diseases. So, don't overdo it on the food delivery, as these meals tend to be higher in things like fat, salt, and sugar. You know, the wickedly good stuff that is unhealthy for us. Here is how you can properly enjoy a dish you didn't make.

Start by figuring out what you want to eat. Trust your cravings. You can order from your favorite restaurant through a food delivery app or by calling directly and picking it up. The latter is recommended, as it saves the restaurant some money. Also, try ordering from a Black-owned business. They deserve your support while supporting you on your feast. Lastly, be sure to put a limit on how often you order takeout. Consider eating out once a week (like, Friday) or a couple times a month. It'll give you something to look forward to if you schedule the days you're eating out.

In short, you deserve a night of enjoying food that will hit the spot. You'll get to spend more time eating and relaxing, rather than cooking and cleaning, as you practice radical self-care.

Make Your Bed

Getting the morning started can sometimes be a struggle, but making your bed gives you a sense of preparedness and is beneficial to your physical and mental health. This activity can be linked to feelings of accomplishment and relaxation. The act of making your bed creates a sense of routine, signaling to yourself it's time to get up and go. It's like crossing off the first thing on our daily to-do list. Making our bed is also a form of tidying up, and research has found that organization is good for our overall health. So, make that bed in the morning so you feel ready to face whatever oppressive nonsense the world throws at you on your journey to radical self-care.

Working this exercise into your morning routine can be as simple as pulling the covers up and propping your pillows on your bed. If you're not used to making your bed, try some of these tips to get you started: Make your bed as soon as you wake up, connect it to a morning activity you usually do (like taking a shower), or create a reminder on your phone or on a sticky note. Just doing it is the key. Eventually, it'll instinctively become part of your morning routine.

After you make your bed, you will be less stressed and more focused. It'll feel good to have at least accomplished one thing before your day gets started, as well as come home to a nicely made bed after a long day. And over time, you will notice your whole being feels balanced and calm. You deserve easy mornings. Get into it.

Buy New Clothes

It's time to take yourself shopping. Buying a new outfit is a great way to shower ourselves with love. When we take time out of our day to shop, we're actively practicing adoration and appreciation of our body. We get to do things like admire the curves of our hips as we try on a pair of pants. In addition, our self-acceptance is found in the dressing room as we explore how different clothing items look on our body. And sis, you need all the body positivity you can get because we know society enjoys criticizing the bodies of Black women. Before heading out to the store, do the following: Make a list of the items you want to buy, create a budget, and select the places you want to shop. Sticking to a shopping plan will help you stay on track. That way, you won't be tempted to deviate from your list and spend more than you intended.

Shopping allows us to tune out the negative messages from the world around our bodies. It's also a pleasurable experience. Literally. Dopamine—the pleasure chemical—is released when we contemplate new purchases. Buying new clothes is good for you, as sometimes you just need a little bit of retail therapy to feel better as you navigate your radical self-care experience. Don't shop until you drop. Shop mindfully, and you'll boost your mood and outlook on life and yourself.

Consume Less Sugar

When it comes to how much sugar we eat, less is better. Sugar is hidden in everything. Next time you buy a food item, check out the nutrition label. You'll be shocked by how many grams of sugar are present. And because sugar is in just about anything, we need to be vigilant about consuming less of it. Sugar is the silent killer for Black women. Too much of it can lead to heart disease and diabetes—two preventable diseases that affect Black women. Not to mention, sugar increases our chance of weight gain, cancer, depression, dental and cognitive deterioration, and acne. How can something so sweet be so bad? Well, it doesn't have to be. Just decrease your sugar intake.

To consume less sugar, try any of these tricks: Swap sodas, energy drinks, juices, and sweetened teas for water or unsweetened seltzer. Instead of using regular sugar or artificial sweetener in your coffee or tea, use agave nectar or honey. Lastly, try to buy products that have no added sugar. Avoiding sugar completely is hard. Your goal should be to simply reduce it.

As you eat less sugar, you'll notice your energy levels will rise and your health will improve. So, put the candy down. Your body deserves this kind of radical self-care.

Plan Your Vacation Days

The fact is your job probably overworks you. Society thrives on burning Black women out. You know, the vibe of let's have you do your job and everybody else's job too. Like you don't already have enough to do. *side-eye* Well, it's time to put this mindset to rest. Literally.

Shift your mind to viewing rest as a necessity, just like your job. You require rest to operate at your utmost best as you embrace this season of radical self-care. Don't let your job rob you of this right.

First, take note of how many days off you're allotted annually. Most jobs give you around ten to fourteen. Release the guilt and take off one or two weeks in your month of choice. Or, be strategic and take one day a month for the whole year. (Try a Monday or Friday.) This day can be like your reset day for the month. However you choose to spend time away from work, just do it. After all, your job is not responsible for your well-being. You are. Take those days off and enjoy them.

So what are you waiting for? Have you planned out your sick, personal, or vacation days for the year? Figuring out when to take some time to rest is good for your body and mind. Do it. When we know our time off from work is approaching, it gives us something to look forward to. Additionally, planning our vacation days prevents our busy schedule from interfering with actually taking time away.

Clean Your Home

Improve your physical health by cleaning up your living space. Life gets busy and sometimes our home can become messy. However, keeping an unkempt living area is detrimental to our body and mind, sis. To make sure your living space stays tidy, try some of these strategies: Clean your home biweekly or at least monthly. Put things away after you use them. Throw out trash weekly—full or not. Wipe down your countertops after you finish cooking. And alternate the rooms you clean every weekend.

Seeing chaos in your home can be exhausting, especially on top of all the day-to-day stressors of being a Black woman. In a messy home, you're constantly reminded of all the work you have to do. How can we rest when we can't visualize a place to relax? Additionally, a messy home spreads things like allergens, germs, and pests. Clutter also creates an unsafe environment, especially if items block doorways. Lastly, a messy living space may cause unhealthy weight gain. If our kitchen is a mess, we will be more likely to engage in unhealthy eating habits, like ordering takeout nightly. Thus, it's time for you to keep your home clean. Or, if you hate cleaning, and have the means to do so, hire someone to come at least once a month.

Ultimately, the benefits of tidying up your living area include reducing stress, fatigue, and illnesses. You already spend most of your time fighting off the effects of societal oppression. Don't let your home be another place where you have to do work. You deserve a peaceful living environment as you spruce up your self-care.

Listen to Your Body

Elevate your self-care by listening to your body. The most important part about taking care of our body is paying attention to its needs. Our body, like our mind, speaks to us. It sends messages when it's hurt. Ever have a body ache you just can't get rid of? That's stress and trauma. Listen closely to the pains and you will know when you have pushed yourself beyond your limits. For example, stress can manifest as tension in your neck, shoulders, and back. If you continue to ignore those signs, it can turn into bigger health issues. So, do your body a favor and act when it sends distress signals.

To better listen to your body, believe whatever you are feeling, acknowledge it, and figure out a remedy. One way to do this is by body mapping your stress; make a note of where you feel aches and pains when you're in distress. Say no to the mindset of Black women being conditioned to push through all types of pain. Simply paying attention to the tension in your body and deciding to do something about it is an act of radical self-care. Choose to be radical, sis.

Essentially, your body wants to be heard and treated well. Just like your mind, it has a memory of its own. It keeps a bank of all the emotional hits it takes and shows up in different ways. Pay attention to what your body is telling you and you will know when it's time to take care of yourself.

Create a Nighttime Skincare Routine

There's just something relaxing about doing a nighttime skincare routine. It's like a nightly mini spa day for ourselves. If you don't have a bedtime beauty regimen, create one. Our skin is the most precious part of our body. Take care of it, and it will take care of you. They say, *Black don't crack*, and that's true if you pamper your skin. There are many ways you can do your nighttime skincare routine, but here you'll find a simple suggested order for radical self-care.

First off, wash your hands. It's important to make sure they're freshly clean before diving into your bedtime beauty routine.

- **Cleanse:** Remove your makeup with a wipe or a cleansing oil. Follow up with a gentle facial cleanser.
- **Tone:** With the toner of your choice, preferably a hydrating one, apply it to your skin with a cotton swab or your hands. Let it completely dry before you jump into the next step.
- **Treatment:** This is where you apply whatever spot treatments you prefer. Normally, these are products you don't want to use daily because they harshly treat things like acne or hyperpigmentation. And if you're in your mid-twenties to early thirties, apply that retinol.
- **Moisturize:** Last step is to use a moisturizer that will keep you hydrated throughout the night.

You'll need to play around and discover which products work best for you. A feeling of calm and relaxation will follow your bedtime skincare routine, which is exactly how you want to feel before you jump into bed.

Sleep on a Silk Pillowcase

Upgrade your bedtime routine by sleeping on a silk pillowcase. As you know, a good night's rest is essential to maintaining our health. Adding a silk pillowcase to your bedding will help elevate your nighttime experience. Not only will you feel like a queen sleeping on such a smooth surface, but you'll also improve the quality of your hair and skin. *Hello, beauty sleep.*

To select the right silk pillowcase for you, you must first know silk is measured in fabric weight called momme. Purchase a pillowcase where the silk is twenty-two momme or higher. You can also get Mulberry silk, which is the highest quality of silk you can buy. And if you're ballin' on a budget, purchase a satin pillowcase; it's made from silk and other materials—the same beauty benefits at a cheaper price.

There are quite a few benefits of owning a silk pillowcase. First, when your bonnet or scarf falls off in the middle of the night, you can sleep without worrying about your hair. The silk pillowcase leaves hair smooth, reducing damage or breakage. Second, your skin will be more hydrated, as silk pillowcases don't soak up as much moisture as cotton.

The silk pillowcase will regulate your body temperature throughout the night while protecting your hair and skin. After one night, you'll never go back to sleeping on cotton. A comfortable and cool night's rest is the kind of beauty sleep you deserve.

Practice Yoga

Yoga is an exercise that has one purpose: to heal our body. It is a series of movements and poses that work together to improve our strength, flexibility, and breathing. These three areas are a dynamic combination for maintaining our physical health.

Begin your venture into a yoga practice by finding a studio to join. Most studios allow a free one-week trial. It might not be possible, but try to find a yoga place that feels inclusive. Sometimes, yoga studios can feel like a place that only welcomes white women. So, prepare yourself for this kind of environment, but don't let it stop you from participating.

If going to a yoga studio is not your style, look for yoga instructors you can learn from online. There are many Black yoga instructors out there who provide yoga with a suggested donation. Most importantly, research and try all kinds of different yoga practices. Pursue yoga until you find one that works for you, because the benefits of practicing yoga include lowering our risk of high blood pressure and heart disease, which tackles illnesses that impact Black women at a higher rate. Additionally, yoga reduces physical and emotional distress like body aches and depression. Including a regular yoga practice into your self-care routine will be good for your overall well-being.

Be gentle with yourself as you practice yoga on your road to radical self-care. It can be challenging if you are new to it. But the more you do yoga, the better you get at it. At the end of your exercise, you will become more self-aware. Yoga forces you to pay attention to your body and your breath. It reminds you to slow down and be kind to yourself. The stressors of the world will fade away once you hit the yoga mat. Inhale. Exhale. Unwind.

Resist Burnout

Contrary to society's popular belief, life as a Black woman does not always have to be associated with struggle. Yes, the environments we're in create situations where we are pushed into working harder than everyone else. However, that doesn't mean we have to buy into the belief that we must burn out to be valued. When we overwork our body by doing things like working after-hours, we're not valuing our rest time. We're putting the needs of others before our own. It can be hard to shift from being a martyr for the sake of everyone else, but you can do it. Here are some tricks on how you can resist burnout:

- **Get an accountability partner(s).** Have people in your circle whose opinion you trust and value. These are people who you are okay with calling you out on your BS, so that when they tell you it's time to tap out, you step back.
- **Create boundaries** around the things you know you have a tendency to overextend yourself with.
- **Don't bring work home.** Allow home time to be for you and you alone. Leave your work at the office. Turn off your work phone or place your work laptop in a room away from you.
- **Rest when your body says so.** If you are tired, do not fight it. Take that nap your body is calling for.

As you work through resisting burnout, your body will thank you. You will reclaim your self-worth and relinquish the need to be validated by overworking yourself for another.

Go to the Hair Salon

Take a break from being your own hairstylist and visit the hair salon. It is such a sacred place. It's where Black women go to be pampered in peace *and* get some good gossip. Some of the best conversations happen when we're in our stylist's chair.

Before you head to the salon, accept that you might be there at least three hours. Pack snacks, drinks, and reading material. Embrace the wait. This is a social event, after all. And whether it's a regular wash/trim or something else, come prepared with knowledge of the hair treatment you want.

The hair salon is a space where we can figuratively and literally let our hair down. We get to be us without pressure to live up to any stereotypes.

However, a trip to the hair salon can also be a laborious event. *Girl, you know.* You get there on time for your appointment and it takes about an hour or two for you to actually be seen by your stylist. But once you're finally in the styling chair, you can enjoy the pampering and gather any hair advice from your stylist you can apply at home. After you're done, be sure to book another appointment three to six months from that date because it's important to get regular trims.

Treating yourself to a salon visit is the kind of self-care you require. You deserve to relax while someone else shows your hair love.

Go Swimming

Swimming is one of the best exercises for a total body workout, making it the perfect self-care activity. When we're stressed or depressed, dipping into a pool for a quick swim is a great way to cleanse our body of any dormant tension. However, Black people aren't known for being swimmers. This is rooted in systemic racism and privilege. Black individuals were often excluded from public pools. The aquatic space was reserved for white people. In America, during segregation times, white people went as far as to pour bleach and acid into pools where Black folks went swimming. This sparked fear, and many Black people stayed away from pools, creating a racial gap in swimming for generations. It's time to dispel the stereotype that Black folks can't swim.

First off, you'll need to take lessons if you do not know how to swim. Lessons can be found at a community center like the YMCA. Next, make sure you have the right gear. Get an appropriate bathing suit, a swim cap, and goggles. Along with these accessories, make sure you buy a shampoo and conditioner that remove chlorine. You'll need to use these products after every swim session because showering immediately afterward is a must. Most importantly, have fun.

In short, swimming is an exhilarating experience for your body. You will feel refreshed and relaxed after a quick dip in a pool. Oh, and all of your muscles will definitely be sore. Be prepared to take it easy afterward, but don't let it keep you from going back.

Get a Massage

Treating yourself to a massage is exactly what your body needs. When's the last time you paid someone to rub the kinks out of your body? If the answer doesn't come quickly to your mind, then you need to do this activity immediately. The benefits of getting a massage are no secret. A great massage helps reduce stress, anxiety, and muscle or joint pain. It has also been known to increase relaxation, energy, and immunity. Check out the following ways to work a massage into your self-care routine.

Foremost, you can book a massage at a parlor near you. There are different kinds of massages, so book a session with one that fits your needs. If paying to have someone rub on your body is too costly, buy a back or handheld massager. Commit to using it a couple times a week on the area of your body where you feel the most pain after a long workday. All in all, massaging our body is the best way to provide our body with instant relief.

Needless to say, you need to get a massage. As a Black woman, we are conditioned to ignoring the distress in our body. A regular massage will help release any tension that's been living in our body.

Floss Your Teeth

Taking care of our body also includes our teeth. The lack of proper dental care, like flossing, can increase your chance of falling prey to a chronic health issue. In addition to brushing our teeth, flossing is a critical part of upkeeping our oral health. It's been found that there is a link between oral hygiene and illnesses like heart disease and diabetes, which Black women have the highest death rate for. Thus, we must take care of our teeth to maintain our physical health.

To start, it's recommended that you floss your teeth twice a day. Cleaning between your pearly whites helps prevent gum disease. Make sure you floss before you brush your teeth; this way plaque and debris will be successfully flushed away. Follow up brushing with a mouthwash for an extra clean feeling. If you have sensitive gums, there may be some bleeding at first, but the more you floss, the less your gums will bleed.

After you floss your teeth and complete your dental care routine, you will feel accomplished knowing that you are taking good care of your oral and physical health. By flossing, you are decreasing your chances of developing any chronic illnesses. That's a win, sis. Celebrate your radical self-care every chance you get.

Check Your Breasts

Keep your health intact by doing a breast self-exam. Regularly checking our breasts for lumps is how we take back the power over our physical health. When it comes to breast cancer, there is a racial disparity. While fewer Black women are diagnosed with the disease, our mortality rate is higher than white women. This is because Black women tend to be diagnosed at a later stage. Prevent this by being proactive. Check your breasts.

Start by looking at your breasts in the mirror. Check to see if there are any signs of a change, such as swelling or a rash. Next, examine your breasts while lying down. Lift one arm up and use the fingers of your opposite hand to rub your breast in a circular motion. Gently feel for any lumps. Repeat with the other side. Afterward, check your breasts while you are sitting or standing. If you feel a lump, do not panic. Many women have noncancerous bumps in their breasts. But make sure you consult with your doctor immediately. If you don't feel anything, then plan to repeat this examination at least once a month.

All in all, it's important to incorporate a breast self-exam into your monthly self-care routine. You will find peace in being ahead of any possible issues with your health as it relates to your radical self-care.

Stand Up at Your Desk

Stand up for your health. Sitting all day at work is causing more harm to our health than we realize. The fact is we are not meant to always be sedentary. Our body needs to move to thrive. Those who spend most of their days sitting have a greater risk of getting heart disease or diabetes. And with these two illnesses being the leading cause of mortality in Black women, it's vital that we seek to spend more time standing than sitting.

There are a couple things you can do to encourage yourself to stand more during the day. First off, you can purchase a standing desk. This is a desk that is positioned higher than normal and is best used when you are standing. Some standing desks are also adjustable and can be shifted for you to use comfortably while you sit. Don't have a standing desk? No problem. Take ten-minute standing breaks every hour. Instead of sitting at your desk to work, stand up. Both suggestions are something that will take time to get used to, but it'll be worth it.

Ultimately, you want to stand up more to get the blood flowing back through your body. You reduce the number of aches in your body whenever you stand instead of sit. It's time to take a stand on your road to radical self-care.

Simplify Wash Day

When it comes to taking care of our hair, less is better. No matter if our hair is natural or relaxed, our tresses require simple techniques to thrive. It's been discovered that an excessive use of hair butters, creams, and oils doesn't always help hydrate Black women's hair. Sometimes, these products act as a barrier for our hair obtaining moisture, and hydration is key to keeping our natural tresses healthy. Simplify your hair care with fewer steps, and you'll look forward to wash day on your journey to radical self-care.

Start by washing your hair with a shampoo of choice at least once a week. After you're done, and your hair is still soaking wet, apply a generous amount of conditioner. Leave it in for the recommended amount of time on the product's instructions. Rinse it out completely and dry your hair with a clean cotton towel. Apply a leave-in conditioner and let your hair air dry. Wash day is done.

By not overloading our tresses with products, we're nourishing our hair with what it needs and giving it room to breathe. You'll see that your hair is just like you: It needs gentle love and care.

Use a Humidifier

Keep your skin and lungs healthy by using a humidifier in your home. A humidifier is a device that adds moisture to dry air. Breathing in dry air can be detrimental to our physical health. It can exacerbate issues like allergies or dry skin. For Black women, this is important to know. Chronic lower respiratory diseases, such as chronic bronchitis, emphysema, and asthma are among the top ten conditions that claim the lives of Black women every year. So, sis, you need to start using a humidifier to improve the air quality in your home and prevent any chronic health issues.

First off, humidifiers come in different sizes. Decide what works best for you and purchase it. Once you get your humidifier, follow all instructions, fill it with purified or distilled water, and use it whenever you want. Hot tip: The best time to use a humidifier is when you are sleeping. To make sure your humidifier operates at its best, be sure to clean it regularly and change out the water daily. If you take care of your humidifier, it will take care of you.

Once you adopt this practice, you will notice that your skin will feel more hydrated and your lungs will feel clearer. Take a deep breath and plan for a better breathing experience on your radical self-care journey.

Buy Cute Pajamas

Obtaining rest is our right. Therefore, make bedtime a special event with cute pajamas. When we spend all day doing our job while combating acts of oppression from people we may or may not know, we deserve a good night's sleep. So purchase pajamas you can't wait to slip into, which makes sleepy time something you can joyfully anticipate. Even if you prefer to "roam free," new loungewear can lift your spirits after a long day. This way, when you tell yourself that you are getting ready for bed, you really are by creating a ritual of changing into something stylish before bed—even if you take it off.

Foremost, decide what kind of pajamas you enjoy. Think about what makes you more comfortable at night. Is it pants, shorts, or a nightgown? Er…um…is it nothing? Once you figure that out, purchase sleepwear that is cute and accommodating (like a robe), making you excited to go to bed. Consider buying at least seven outfits, or maybe three robes, so that you are covered for the week. *Pun intended.* Additionally, make changing into your nightwear the first step of your nighttime routine. It'll get your body and mind prepared to wind down for bed. Slip 'em on (or off) and enjoy your restful evening.

Purchasing cute pajamas helps make rest a priority in your life. Make the change; your body needs it for your many nights of restful radical self-care.

Communicate Your Needs

Communicating our needs is a healing activity for our body. Needs are things that help us function as the best version of ourselves, making us feel fully supported. When we suppress our words, thoughts, and emotions, it can manifest in our body as illnesses, pains, and aches. As a Black woman, we've been conditioned to keep quiet about our desires, as well as things that hurt us mentally and physically. We're taught through situations that if we speak up, there are consequences—like losing our job or being ignored. So, we don't share how we want to be treated and accept whatever falls into our lap. Nah. This ain't the way to live. It's time to communicate your needs and not apologize for it.

Start by recognizing what exactly you need from different areas in your life. If this is something another person can help you obtain, like a supervisor, friend, partner, or family member, express it to them. Uncommunicated needs breed resentment of undiscussed expectations. On the other hand, if you have a need you can satisfy, tell yourself. Acknowledge this support that you can provide yourself and do it. This can look like telling yourself you need a nap—and actually taking one. It's crucial to communicate your needs so you can live at ease in your body.

After you share the things you need to feel supported, you will be calmer with your body feeling less agitated. Communicating your needs is an empowering act that you need to practice today on your discovery of radical self-care.

Get Your Hair Braided

Braids look so darn good on Black women. First off, let's make this clear: Black women invented braids. (*I said what I said.*) Decide what kind of braided style you want, and then treat yourself to a nice protective style and a wonderful cultural experience.

As Black women, getting our hair braided is an ancient practice that originated with African people. Different patterns and styles were used as ways to identify things like someone's tribe, power, or age. Generations bonded as women and children learned to braid each other's hair. The purpose of braids has since evolved to be mainly used for hair styling and protecting purposes. Cornrows provide us with a cute low manipulation style, and box braids allow us to protect our natural hair. And while braids are beautifully connected to our cultural identity, they have been culturally appropriated and ridiculed by non-Black people. (*Make that make sense, somebody!*) Nevertheless, we always look cute in braids. So take some time off and go get your hair braided.

Start by connecting with someone who can braid hair. If you're lucky, you'll have a friend or family member who can help you out. Otherwise, try and find someone through word of mouth, via social media, or with a hair stylist booking app. Get your hair did and enjoy your new look. After you get your hair braided, you'll feel fabulous and closer to your ancestral roots as you continue your radical self-care experience.

Lotion Your Whole Body

Lotioning your whole body is a simple self-care exercise. Treat your skin right by lathering yourself entirely with lotion. *Body butter works too.* This self-care activity has one purpose: to nourish your skin. It's also probably something you were taught to do as a child. You might have had a Black mama who made sure you put lotion all over your body (and baby powder all over your chest, if you grew up in the South) after taking a bath or shower. Prevent your skin from becoming dry and developing other issues simply by applying lotion to your whole body.

Start off by finding a brand that works for you. It might take some trial and error to discover which one your skin loves. Next, make sure you apply lotion to your body immediately after taking a bath or shower, especially your feet. It's the best time to provide your body with premium moisture. Last, reapply lotion throughout the day if you need it because you don't want to walk around ashy—particularly your hands (and elbows if visible). After you nourish your skin with lotion, your skin will be soft, and you will feel loved. Take care of your skin, and it will take care of you on your path to radical self-care.

Try Fasting

Rejuvenate your body and clear your mind by fasting. To put it plainly, a fast is when you stop eating for a certain period. It can last twelve to twenty-four hours, but some can last several days. The benefit of withholding food from our body is that it can improve things like cholesterol levels and blood pressure, bettering the function of our heart. Additionally, it's been known to help people with diabetes, which we know disproportionately impacts the lives of Black women. The purpose of going on a fast is not to lose weight, although weight loss may happen. It's to reset your body.

Foremost, consult with a physician beforehand, as there are many ways to complete a fast. First, you can abstain from eating completely for a designated amount of time. Next, you can eliminate only certain kinds of foods (meat, sugar, etc.) for a specific period. Last, you can restrict your eating to between a specific time slot: say, noon and eight p.m. You must find what works for you. Consider picking one day a week to abstain from food for a couple hours of radical self-care healing. For example, not eating any food until noon on Sundays. If you choose to fast, be sure to stay hydrated with water.

All in all, fasting not only helps our physical health. It also aids our mental and spiritual wellness. By withholding food from our body for a certain amount of time, we allow our entire being to clear itself from distraction and impurities for a total body cleanse.

Treat Yourself to a Manicure and Pedicure

It's time to pamper yourself with a trip to the nail salon. Getting a manicure and pedicure is a self-care activity that never fails to make us feel better. Taking time out of our day to have our nails cleaned, cut, and painted to our liking allows our body the period of rest it needs on the road to radical self-care discovery. Peace is discovered as you have your feet massaged. Relaxation is activated when your hands are lathered with lotion. And most importantly, power is found in the freedom of choosing how you want your fingernails and toenails to be designed. Treat yourself to a manicure and pedicure as soon as possible.

To make your mani-pedi experience worthwhile, start by booking your appointment ahead of time. If you can, locate a Black-owned nail salon. It's important to support any Black-owned beauty shops to avoid being met with anti-Blackness while you're trying to de-stress. Next, consider bringing the nail polish you want to use, as well as any base or topcoat you would prefer the nail technician to apply. Once you're at the nail salon, relax and enjoy your nail treatments. You deserve to take a load off and be pampered.

After you get a manicure and pedicure, you will feel beautiful and relaxed. It'll feel good to take care of your hands and feet—two pairs of body parts that you use every day and that carry a lot of your stress.

Plan a Self-Care Day

When it comes to practicing self-care, it is important to designate days where we do absolutely nothing but take care of ourselves. Life can really beat us down. Our daily interaction with society constantly sends us the message that Black women don't matter. And because of this, we require days we can devote to escaping from the world and doing what makes us feel good. The purpose of a day dedicated to your wellness is to help counteract any tension or pain that is held up in your body as a result of stress. Hence, the need for you to plan a self-care day.

On this day, you do whatever you feel is best for you. Perhaps it's running errands you just can't seem to get done on the weekends. Maybe you sleep in and spend the day reading a book. Or, you could plan a full day of spa treatments. Whatever suits your self-care needs, just do it.

After your self-care day, you will feel relaxed and refreshed, ready to face whatever the world throws your way. Your body's stress signals will return to their baseline, with your mind and body having less visible signs of stress as you move farther along your radical self-care journey.

Adjust Your Caffeine Consumption

Caffeine is great. It helps keep us alert and awake. However, too much can be bad for our physical wellness. If we plan to get a good night's rest, then we need to monitor how much we consume. Otherwise, we could experience digestive issues or headaches. And because the effects of caffeine can last up to twelve hours in the body, it's important to stop having it at least six hours before bed. After a long day of dealing with microaggressions, not being able to sleep because of caffeine is not ideal. Thus, we need to adjust our caffeine consumption.

To start, pay attention to what you're drinking or eating that has caffeine. Coffee and tea are known for their caffeine amount, but don't forget about soda, energy drinks, and chocolate. Next, make sure you don't have more than 400 milligrams of caffeine daily. Keep count of the cups of coffee, tea, soda, etc. If you notice that you consume a lot, reduce it by one cup each day. Caffeine has an impact on your body, and it's important to be aware of this.

Switching up your allotted daily caffeine can be hard. As you do this, you may experience caffeine withdrawal symptoms that can include body aches and fatigue. However, the less caffeine you consume on your journey to radical self-care, the better rest you will get at night and the more energy you will have during the day.

Hug Someone

Boost your physical wellness by hugging someone you love. There's just something calming about a warm embrace from another person. The skin-to-skin contact is good for our health because it has many benefits. Hugging causes our body to release all types of feel-good hormones, including dopamine, serotonin, and oxytocin. Dopamine is responsible for making us feel pleasure, serotonin's job is to make us feel happy, and oxytocin is famous for sending feelings of love throughout our body. Getting a hug also decreases feelings of loneliness, stress, and anxiety. Hugging is kind of a big deal and an activity we must add to our daily self-care routine.

To reap the benefits of a hug, cuddle someone you love and trust for at least twenty seconds. When you stay in an embrace that long, your cortisol (stress hormone) decreases, and all those aforementioned feel-good hormones are released. You can find a friend and hug it out in the name of self-care. Or, consider working this into your regular greeting with friends and family members. It'll change your wellness and your relationships.

Life as a Black woman in this world can have you feeling lonely, stressed, and anxious—all the time. On top of having to deal with the distress of race- and gender-based discriminations on a regular basis, you can feel isolated and as if you have to go through your struggles alone. Hugging someone reminds you that you are loved and that you can practice self-love as often as you'd like in the name of radical self-care.

Part 3
SOUL

When it comes to taking care of ourselves, our soul or spirit plays an integral part in our overall well-being. Our spirit represents the essence of who we are as a person. Practicing self-care for our soul encourages us to get in touch with our inner being. The vibration of our spirit speaks volumes about our wellness; the goal is to vibrate at a high level—above the mess that's trying to bring us down. And when we're vibrating at a chaotic or low pace, we need the exercises in this section. In the following pages, you will find activities that will help you operate as your highest self, and you will build a deeper connection with yourself, the people in your life, and the world around you.

Learn Your Family's History

Building a connection to our ancestral lineage is one of the most empowering things we can do for our spirit. It is the exercise of learning more about the history and culture of our family of origin. *Alexa, play "Bigger" by Beyoncé.* To begin connecting to your family's heritage, retrieve stories from family members about your ancestral history. Schedule a phone call or visit with an elder (parents, grandparents, etc.). Once you gather information, learn more about the land and culture of your people through research. Continue uncovering the many layers of your people; there's much to be learned.

Journeying back to our roots allows us to get a sense of belonging. Sometimes, as Black women, we feel isolated. We're often surrounded by others who don't look like us. It can cause us to question the purpose of our existence and feel disconnected from others who look like us, our tribe. Many Black women are descendants of enslaved people with a disjointed connection to the Motherland, Africa. However, this self-care practice is not only for those who are unsure of their African identity. It is an activity that all Black people can do. Whether you're a mixed Black woman, a daughter of Black immigrants, a Black Latina, etc., discovering where you come from helps you gain a better understanding of yourself.

After you do this activity, do not be surprised if you have a greater sense of pride. We come from a strong line of people who thrived, despite the attempted cultural destruction by colonization.

Create a Morning Playlist

Your morning helps set the tone for your day. Silent mornings aren't your thing? That's okay. Sometimes, we need to turn on some music when we wake up to prepare our spirit for the day. For your morning playlist, it's important to pick songs that are empowering. Research has found that listening to music can help us cope with negative emotions like feelings of depression. Your morning playlist is like the body armor you put on to protect your spirit from the nonsense the world will throw at you. You need this. Listening to mood-boosting music is the perfect way to start your day.

Fill your day with music you love that also makes you feel loved. Some song suggestions for your playlist include "Golden" by Jill Scott, "Holy" by Jamila Woods, and "Brown Skin Girl" by Beyoncé, Blue Ivy, SAINt JHN, and WizKid. You can listen to the music as you get ready in the morning or on your way to wherever you're headed for the day. Enjoy your good morning mood.

As a result of listening to your morning playlist, you'll be ready to face your day. Your spirit will be in an uplifted mood and protected from any microaggressions that try to bring you down as you navigate through a day of radical self-care.

Listen to Your Intuition

Your intuition is the guiding light inside you. It's that voice that helps you make decisions. The one that tells you when something just doesn't feel right. As children, we're taught to not listen to our intuition and instead let the adults around us make decisions for us. As Black women, the media, society, and our own communities teach us to not listen to our intuition by telling us how we should behave to get the results we want in our work life, love life, etc. *Wait ninety days to give up the cookie and they'll commit.* And if it feels like your intuition is a bit wonky, know she hasn't gone anywhere. You just need to practice listening to her more, releasing any mistrust you have of yourself. Because to not listen to your intuition is to not trust yourself. It's to not trust your ability to handle your decisions as a result of listening to yourself. There will always be good or bad consequences to not listening to our intuition. Whether it's with a feeling or a circumstance, we must trust that little voice inside. Here's how to practice listening to your intuition more:

- **Go to a quiet place.** This can be through meditation, a walk, prayer, or another activity. Clearing the noise from outside your head will allow you to create space and listen to what your mind is telling you.
- **Make decisions without consulting other people for their opinion.** There's a time to hear what other people have to say. But when it comes to decisions that only impact you,

consult with yourself. Do what feels right to you and not what feeds the narrative of how you want others to perceive you.

- **Trust your initial feeling about anything.** Start small, like with which outfit you'll wear today, and go with it. Embrace the negative and positive feelings. Those emotions serve as signals that provide your brain with information about what you do and don't like. Honor those feelings going forward.
- **Forgive yourself for the times you ignored your intuition.** You didn't know better then. Now, you do. Make daily vows to listen to your inner voice.

It takes practice to trust your gut feeling. However, the more you do it, the more distinct your inner voice will become to you as you progress on your road to radical self-care

Relax with Aromatherapy

Aromatherapy is the practice of using essential oils, through smell and skin absorption, to improve our health. It is especially helpful with decreasing feelings of stress and anxiety within our body. Some other benefits of aromatherapy include boosting immunity, improving quality of sleep, and managing pain. If you've never used essential oils as a way to take care of yourself, that's okay. Let go of your daily troubles by relaxing with aromatherapy. Following are some tips to get started.

Before you start using essential oils, research to find out which ones you want to use. With over one hundred different kinds of oils out there, it's important to know the uses for each of them. Peppermint, eucalyptus, and lavender are a great place to start. All three have wonderful healing properties. Got a headache? Rub peppermint oil on your temples. Want to fall asleep easily? Put a couple droplets of eucalyptus oil in your aromatherapy diffuser at bedtime. Have sore muscles and joints? Slather lavender oil on the pain area. The use of essential oils allows us to peacefully take control of our own radical self-care.

Whenever you use aromatherapy, you're encouraging your body to heal itself. You will feel better after using essential oils to decompress from the world's oppressive measures. The power is in your hands.

Visit Your Ancestors' Land

There's something magical about connecting to the land of our ancestors. Walking the same spaces as the people of the generations before us allows us to build a closer connection to our cultural identity. It helps us get a better understanding of our family's history and the African diaspora, which reminds us that globally, Black people are interconnected. Moreover, traveling to a place where those in your bloodline lived is an unforgettably tangible experience for your spirit.

First off, your ancestors' land is anywhere your family has lived. Whether it's where you currently live or where your family emigrated, this self-care activity is unique to your history. Perhaps it's taking an ancestry DNA test where you discover that you're a certain percentage of a West African country. Plan a trip to that place. Or, maybe your family moved to a different country or state than the one your parents or grandparents were raised in. Go visit that area and learn about the culture. Complete this journey however you see fit.

Ultimately, as a Black woman, the story of your ancestors is not a monolith. It is your unique experience. And after you finish your excursion, you will have a better sense of self. Pride and assurance will fill your soul as you enhance your radical self-care experience.

Schedule a Friend Date

Each friendship we have is different, but it is a necessity for our soul to schedule a friend date. Linking up with a friend helps us reconnect with ourselves. A good friend is someone with whom we have a good spiritual connection. They are also a person who cares deeply for us. Someone we can confide in and vice versa.

First off, life can get busy, so planning a hangout with a friend may not always be easy. Collaborate with your friend to come up with a master plan to always make time for each other. Try scheduling monthly meetups or commit to regularly communicating days and times that work best for the two of you.

Ultimately, it is important that you have at least one strong friendship. The world can feel like a lonely place for a Black woman, and a true friend can be our safe space. Some of the best relationships you'll ever have won't be with a romantic partner; they'll be with a close friend. And like any relationship, a friendship bond requires the two parties to continue building on their initial connection.

Your spirit will thank you for this friend date. You'll feel grounded and lighthearted afterward. A friendship date is the exact kind of radical self-care activity you need to boost your energy and mood. Reach out to that friend you've been thinking about while reading this.

Stop Being a "Ride or Die"

Girl. You need to let go of being the "ride or die" in all your relationships. A woman who is a "ride or die" is someone who will do whatever for a person they love. This can be a partner, friend, or family member. Usually, it means you exhibit an extreme loyalty that can also lead you into dangerous situations. It also means abandoning your intuition, as well as dignity of self. If you are proud of being a "ride or die," ask yourself: *Where are you going and why do you gotta die?* This trait is typically expected from Black women. Now is your chance to say no to this mentality. Be loyal to yourself for a better radical self-care journey.

First, stop seeking relationships where you can act as a savior to an individual. Find connections where the energy you put out is reciprocated. Part of the reason you may like being a "ride or die" is that it allows you to feel needed. This feeds codependency, which is a sign of an unhealthy relationship. Second, begin to listen to your intuition more and walk away or say no to things that make you uncomfortable. Lastly, end any relationships where your loyalty is used as a way to control your actions.

When you relinquish the "ride or die" mindset, you encourage yourself to put your desires first. The energy from your soul summons healthy relationships to enter your life.

Find a Mentor in Your Industry

No matter what industry we work in, we need a mentor—ideally, someone who is Black. A mentor is someone who can offer us guidance and insight as we navigate our career. The benefit of having a mentor is that we have someone on our side who has done what we are trying to achieve. This person can offer advice on how to reach our goals, as well as be a confidant for any work-related issues. Black women are often second-guessed and left behind in the workplace. Being connected to a mentor will help you feel like you are not wading through the career waters alone. Follow these steps to get a mentor in your work field.

Start off by researching your industry. Be on the lookout for someone whose career steps you admire. If you're a college student, this can be a recent graduate who is working in your future field or another junior level individual. Already in your career? Try to find someone who is more senior at your workplace or at a level above you but in a different company. Next step is to connect with this person. The best way to do this is via email. Or, at an industry event and with a follow-up email. When you reach out to the potential mentor, be sure to do it with the intention of building a working relationship and not looking for a job. (Psst: Job offers come from relationships, anyway.) Be aware of the busy schedule the person might have and wait for them to respond. Follow up if needed in an appropriate time frame. Be aware that finding the right mentor might take time. Don't rush the process. It will be worth the patience you exhibit on your journey to radical self-care.

Locating a mentor in your industry is essential to maintaining career stamina. With a mentor on your side, you will feel anchored in your work. Thus, you'll be able to better fight off incidents of impostor syndrome.

Date Yourself

Start dating yourself by making note of the things you like. Create space for yourself to take yourself out on dates to the movies or dinner. It's important for you to get comfortable with spending time alone, understanding that you are not lonely. If you are single, you are giving your soul a gift. For many Black women, being single is a way of life.

It's been reported that Black women are less likely to get married or be in a relationship than women of other races. However, being single is not a curse. When we are single, we get to make ourselves the main priority, focusing on our dreams and desires. Needless to say, there's nothing wrong with wanting a romantic relationship. It's when we center our entire life around finding or being in a relationship that it becomes problematic for our spirit. So, enjoy singlehood while you can and treat yourself like you're the biggest catch. The more you do that, the more you will become in tune with your likes and dislikes. Then, when you do get into a relationship, you will have solidified self-assurance and mastered self-awareness on your discovery of radical self-care.

If you are already in a relationship, you can still take time to date yourself. Be sure to carve out time away from your partner for just you, and get to know and nurture yourself outside the context of your relationship.

Plan a Girls Trip

There's something exhilarating about traveling to a new place with our favorite girlfriends. We get to experience new adventures with friends we love, build stronger bonds, and catch up on life. Many moons ago it wasn't safe for Black people to travel together in groups. But now, embrace the freedom of getting to take a trip with your chosen sisterhood.

The key to having a successful girls trip is structure and freedom. *Say what? How's that possible?* It's easy. First, pick a place that none of you have ever visited. Plan the accommodations accordingly, like picking a resort and everyone books on their own or getting a hotel room and you all split the costs. Next, decide what kind of trip you guys will be having. Is it a turnup or turndown vacation? Everybody needs to have the same vibe. In addition, make sure you stay connected on your trip. Create a group chat and plan standing dinners or breakfasts. This way, everybody has a space to check in and plan the daily adventures. Lastly, make sure you all go on at least one group adventure, like a guided tour. You will want to make sure everybody has one memorable moment with the group, as traveling with your girlfriends is one of the most replenishing things you can do for your soul. Book your trip now and revive your spirit for a new level of radical self-care. When you return, you will most likely crave another one because your spirit will be refreshed and at peace.

Buy an Indoor Plant

Owning an indoor plant is good for our spiritual health. It encourages us to build a better connection to the world around us, as well as get in touch with our African roots. Agricultural practices are native to our ancestral homelands. Our people lived off the land they were either stolen from, shipped to, or colonized on for centuries. Engaging with plant life is indigenous to Black people, but modern times has ripped us away from greenery.

Additionally, there are benefits to having a plant baby. Plants help reduce indoor air pollutants by absorbing toxins and producing oxygen. They are also known to decrease stress and improve mood. And most certainly, they provide us with an outlet to give mindfulness care. When we tend to our plant's needs by providing it with the proper amount of water, sun, etc., we are mirroring care that we should give back to ourselves. Having a plant is a necessity for our wellness.

To begin your plant mama path, visit a plant nursery. There you can connect with a plant professional who can guide you on the kind of houseplant you should purchase. Getting a snake plant is a great place to start. It is simple to take care of and won't die easily on you, so you can continue to build your green thumb confidence. As you get further in your indoor plant ownership, do your research to maintain your plant's health. You can also join an online community of Black plant owners to get tips on how to manage your plant baby. Enjoy the journey.

All in all, owning a plant is a rewarding spiritual experience. You are creating a deeper connection with yourself, your ancestors, and the world. As you take care of your plant, feelings of pride and peace will consume your soul. You build a spiritual connection to your plant that betters your health and increases your radical self-care.

Release Limiting Friendships

Sometimes, we have to let go of certain friendships in order to grow. Part of our soul self-care work is knowing when something or someone no longer deserves a place in our life. It's easier said than done.

Friendship breakups are one of the hardest things to go through, but they're an important act of discernment for our spiritual growth. Still, you may not know you are involved in a friendship with someone whose energy is bringing you down.

To figure out if you are friends with someone who is limiting your growth, note that they may have the following characteristics. They might display emotional immaturity, with a specific inability to communicate clearly or be happy for you. This person is also usually fussy about things, with a compulsive need to complain. Nothing ever seems to make them satisfied. Most importantly, your energy will be drained after spending time with them. If someone in particular comes to mind, you need to let this friendship go.

After you do this, you may miss that person. It is part of the process. Be sure to mourn that friendship and trust yourself that you made the right decision. As a Black woman, we can be made to feel like we must remain in relationships that do more harm than good. Sis, you're a goddess and need all the spiritual assistance you can get. You have no room for friendships that limit your journey to wholeness or radical self-care.

Change Your Environment

Sometimes, the thing that's blocking our spiritual growth and healing is the environment we are in. When Black women feel stagnant and like our life is not progressing, we need to remove ourselves from whatever unhealthy space we are inhabiting. The fact is our soul is impacted by our surrounding environment. Change it so you can experience improved spiritual health.

Foremost, you must decide if there is an area in your life where you crave growth but feel stagnant. Next, examine that particular part of your life. Make note of your own actions. Are you doing the same things and expecting a new result? Or, are you looking for improvement in a space that has nothing to serve you? If you answered yes, then you gotta go. Switching up your surroundings can look like moving away from the town where you grew up to discover your passions away from a familiar space. It can also look like quitting your job that continues to deliver disrespect because of your race and gender. You sometimes need to physically change spaces to take care of your soul.

In short, you cannot expect to grow magnificently in unhealthy soil. When the atmosphere around you is damaging to your soul, staying will do more harm than good. Let go of fear, sis. Notice when your environments are toxic for your spirit and give yourself permission to make a plan to exit.

Visit the Beach

Reconnect to yourself by visiting a beach. It is the perfect activity to do when our spirit needs to be uplifted. Feeling the sea breeze on our skin is healing for our soul. Smelling the salty air and hearing the thrashing waves is rejuvenating for our spirit. Peace within is found when our feet are nestled into the sand and our skin is cleansed by the seawater. So, next time you are feeling distressed or out of it, take a trip to the beach.

To work visiting the beach into your self-care routine, consider going at either sunrise or sunset. These magical hours are when it is best to connect with the sun. Your spirit will be inspired by its beauty. If you're unable to go at these times, plan a trip by yourself or with some friends. Make it a whole day if you don't live close to the beach. Plan for a relaxing trip, where you may take a short dip in the water, read a book in a beach chair, or sunbathe on a towel. (Remember your sunscreen!) Either way, get yourself to a beach as soon as possible. Heading there is a great way to release stress and reconnect with yourself as you discover more radical self-care opportunities.

Develop an Abundance Mindset

How we think impacts the way our life looks and feels. Black women are often encouraged to have a scarcity mindset instead of an abundance mindset. We are made to think that other Black women are our competition to attain achievements; this is scarcity thinking. Meanwhile, abundance thinking says there is enough room and resources for everybody to win. Choosing to live an abundant life allows your spirit to feel free. Additionally, it gives you permission to pursue a life filled with great ease—a life that doesn't center around struggle.

To develop an abundance mindset, you need to first get real with yourself by examining your thoughts and actions. Look at the areas in your life where you crave growth, such as your work, love, and family life. Ask yourself, *Am I operating in fear or faith?* If your answer is fear, then explore the why behind it. In addition, commit to disrupting any scarcity thoughts that may arise. Operating in abundance is an ongoing process. You have to work hard to shake off the ways of living with a mentality of lack.

As you practice having an abundance mindset, you will begin to shift the way you view yourself and your life. You will feel content with your choices and less anxious about your future. Gaining an abundant mentality is the key to unlocking a new level of spiritual wellness on your radical self-care journey.

Watch Something Funny

Fill your spirit with joy by watching something funny. To practice this self-care activity, simply go to your favorite streaming website and cruise the comedy section. Pick something funny that you're familiar with or give a new TV show or movie a chance to make you chuckle. Suggested viewing: a stand-up comedy special. But if you're not into comedy specials, watch whatever fits your sense of humor. Allow the joy of laughing to fill your soul and your space on your discovery of radical self-care often.

Laughter is truly the best medicine for our overall wellness. It's been found that laughing has the ability to unleash endorphins (your body's feel good chemicals), protect your heart by increasing blood flow, burn calories, and halt any feelings of anger. Laughter can also bridge the gap between us and others. Who knew watching something funny could be so good for you? And sis, this is exactly what you need to release any stress, anxiety, or anger caused by your daily dose of racial discrimination.

While laughter is great for our physical and mental health, it's our soul that ultimately reaps all the benefits. You'll feel your spirit get lighter as you laugh. Anything that is causing you distress will fly away from your soul with each breathy chuckle.

Create a Financial Plan

Get your money right by creating a financial plan. Our financial health is just as important as our physical, mental, and spiritual wellness. Leveling up on our financial literacy is essential to our life experience as a Black woman. For too long, Black people and their communities around the world have been deprived of financial resources. But that stops with you. Educating yourself on money will empower you to make financial decisions that encourage spiritual stability. Hence, the need to create a financial plan that works for you.

Foremost, you will need to release any guilt or shame you are holding about your current financial habits. You're doing the best you can with whatever knowledge you have. Next, begin to educate yourself on basic money concerns, such as saving. Connect with a professional or read books that speak to the kind of financial guidance you are seeking. Last, but not least, create your financial plan based on advice you have received or researched.

As you work through your financial plan, you'll want to be gentle with yourself. Money comes with a lot of spiritual baggage. It controls the way the world moves. However, it doesn't have to control you. Map your road to financial freedom through managing radical self-care.

Travel Solo

Traveling alone is a surefire way to learn more about yourself. It's also the best way to explore other places and cultures. When we travel alone, we are encouraged to only spend time doing things that spark our own interest. There's no friend or family member dictating your travel itinerary. It's a liberating experience for your soul. But as a Black woman, traveling solo comes with its ups and downs. If you're in another country, people may constantly ask to take pictures with you because it's like they've never seen a Black person before. Don't do it for safety reasons, and also because you're not an animal at a zoo that people can take photos with whenever they please. On the contrary, Black women are treated like queens in other cultures. Our spirit needs to experience this kind of doting. Here are some tips to enjoy your solo travel trip.

Foremost, pick a safe place you have never been. Select your travel dates and book your flight. Plan your accommodations and get excited about your trip. Next, keeping safety in mind, make sure loved ones know where you are going. Share your itinerary with them. Consider using your smartphone to share your location indefinitely with someone you trust. Additionally, consider joining an online solo traveling community to get other travel tips. Most importantly, enjoy your time away.

The more you travel solo, the more you build a deeper connection to yourself and the world around you as you experience radical self-care.

Support Black-Owned Businesses

There are so many benefits to pouring our money into Black-owned companies. By supporting a Black-owned business, we are assisting in building up the Black community, creating jobs for people, closing the racial wealth gap, empowering the local community, and celebrating Black culture. Black-owned businesses are important because Black people have always had to create our own way to survive in this world. Implicit bias prevents us from climbing up the corporate ladder at a quicker pace than our white counterparts, so we have to create our own profitable space. And even if you're not a business owner yourself, you can support those who are attempting to build something that lasts.

Build a deeper connection to the collective Black community by supporting Black-owned businesses. To begin, start locally. Think about businesses you usually visit, like a coffee shop, nail salon, or restaurant. Then, research to see if there is an equivalent of that business that is owned by a Black person in your neighborhood. You can also search online and find curated lists of Black-owned businesses. Whether in person or on the Internet, go spend your money there.

When we support a Black-owned business, we are building a deeper spiritual connection to the Black community. We are a link in the chain that is creating something strong for the next generation of Black people. A sense of Black pride will fill your soul. Your money is going to a space that ethically aligns with your essence. This will further enhance your journey to radical self-care.

Build a Healthy Sisterhood

Creating strong friendships with other women is essential to maintaining our spiritual health. However, we must practice good discernment when building our sisterhood. Having a collective of hand-picked women we can call our sisters provides us with divine protection and projection. We protect our soul from damage when we have spiritually healthy women pouring into us. We progress to our higher self when we connect to other women who are also striving to elevate themselves. We, my sistahs, are women who understand the value of wellness. This is called a healthy sisterhood, and as a Black woman, you must make sure you have your tribe. They are who will help you survive the oppressive world.

First off, you can meet women whom you connect with on a spiritual basis in spaces like a place of faith, school, a group fitness class, or an event of a shared interest. Next, it's important to know the signs of a healthy relationship. This includes respecting each other's differences and similarities, supporting one another's endeavors, being understanding of the other person's time and space, and communicating openly without judgment. If you have any friendships with these characteristics, hold on to them. This is a bond that will continue to propel you forward in life.

No question, building a healthy sisterhood is important to maintaining our overall health. When we engage with women who constantly uplift and support us, we will feel empowered to knock out all our goals, including those for radical self-care.

Reconnect to Your Higher Power

One of the strongest ways to take care of our spiritual health is to reconnect to our Higher Power. This can be a symbol of faith like Jesus Christ or Allah, or another representation of spirituality like the Universe. Wherever we harness our spiritual strength from is who or what we should be finding our way back to.

Foremost, you must recognize that your connection to your Higher Power is a personal relationship. How and when you interact with it should not be dictated by others. One way to reconnect to the higher being is through prayer, which comes in many forms. Prayer can include a more structured practice, or it can simply be you having a conversation with the Higher Power you subscribe to. Another way to re-engage is by congregating with others who share your same beliefs, like in a place of worship or a similar meetup. Being around others who share your same spiritual affinity will encourage you to stay close to your Higher Power. Lastly, consider listening to spiritual music that aligns with your higher connection. The music will invigorate your soul, filling you up with peace and a reminder of your spiritual relationship. Ultimately, it's very important that you reconnect in a way that works for you.

Reuniting with our Higher Power is the perfect activity to do when we're feeling out of whack with ourselves and need clarity or direction.

After you spend time reuniting with your Higher Power, you will feel grounded. To keep this feeling, you must frequently engage in this activity. The world will constantly try to control how you should present yourself to society as a Black woman. However, reconnecting to your Higher Power leads you back to your inner strength, self-worth, and confidence. You won't be moved by the ways of the world as you continue on your road to radical self-care.

Make a Gratitude Jar

A gratitude jar is a jar (or box) filled with reminders of things we are grateful for. When we operate from a place of thanksgiving, we give ourselves permission to focus on the good things in our lives versus the bad. The struggles we face while being a Black woman can sometimes try to take up more space in our lives than they should. We find it easier to focus on our issues than our successes. However, it's better to have the wonderful things in our lives to take hold of our spirit. Making a gratitude jar is an intentional way to shift your inner being to an elevated level in times of distress.

To create your gratitude jar, start by finding a glass jar or sturdy box you want to use. You can purchase one from a craft store or use a recycled item. Next, decorate it however you want. Follow up with using tiny pieces of paper to write down one or two things you are grateful for. You'll want to do this fun self-care activity at least once or twice a week. Or, anytime something special happens that fills you with gratitude, jot it down and throw it in your jar. Soon (or later) your jar will be filled. Then, you'll want to mix up the papers and read at least one note every week to encourage you on your radical self-care journey.

Celebrate the Black Women in Your Life

It's important to give our loved ones their flowers while they are still alive. There are so many ways to celebrate a sistah. You can put together a small gathering following a recent accomplishment, send a gift or flowers, show her love on social media, or something else you feel will fit her personality. All that matters is you show her the love she deserves.

Celebrating the people in our life for their small or big wins helps make our relationships stronger. Our soul needs connection with others to thrive. When we show our friends love for their accomplishments, we send the message that they are valued. Showing love to another Black woman deepens our bond with the collective sistah-hood. And while society is doing the opposite, making a Black woman feel less than for existing, you must be a light and uplift her with love and support. When you do this, your spirit will be filled with pure joy. Giving love to another person intrinsically makes you feel loved as well. The energy you put out is exactly what will be returned to you. Showing love to another Black woman is not just about being kind to her—it's good for your own spiritual wellness and radical self-care.

Show Yourself Compassion

In a world that is harsh on Black women, be gentle with yourself. In many spaces, we're expected to overwork for approval or success while watering down our identity to receive fair treatment or to not be seen as a threat. We're asked to put the needs of others before our own. We're told to show grace for those who discriminate against us while we suffer in silence. It's exhausting. All we want is a well-balanced life filled with ease and love. And when the world will not offer us any sympathy, we must be the ones to show ourselves the compassion we deserve.

Being compassionate toward yourself requires you to be warm and understanding of your humanity. You will have to release any self-judgment. This can look like being kind to yourself when you repeat a habit you are trying to break. Or, not beating yourself up when you seemingly fail at something. You might feel like you don't deserve compassion because society tells you that you aren't allowed to make mistakes as a Black woman. You must let go of self-criticism and have more compassion for yourself. This is an ongoing practice. Do it daily.

As you practice this radical self-care activity, you will notice your feelings of anxiety and stress will decrease. Your spirit will feel lifted, as it will not be weighed down by negative self-talk. Compassion warms your soul and welcomes inner healing. Give yourself permission to enjoy it.

Stop Dating People Who Fetishize Black Women

Dating as a Black woman can be a struggle. Many people love Black women, but they don't actually like *a* Black woman. You know what I mean, sis, especially if you've ever been involved with a man who had a Black woman fetish. *Yuck.* A racial fetish is not just having a preference or type. It's when we're reduced to simply being desired for our racial identity.

To stop dating people who fetishize you, you need to recognize the signs. If the person isn't Black and they tell you "I only date Black women," run. If you hear "I've never dated a Black woman. You're my first," run. If you're told "You're so exotic," run. And if the person doesn't seem to ever call you by your name, but instead prefers to refer to you as adjectives like "beautiful" or "gorgeous," run. None of these are compliments, but major red flags that you're being fetishized.

A person with a Black woman fetish will never see us for our humanity or individuality. They'll only see you for the sexual or romantic gratification you can provide them. Stay away from these kinds of folks. Not being romantically involved with people who fetishize us doesn't mean don't date outside of our race. Date whoever you want. Just be aware of when you're being valued for your racial identity and not for your true essence.

Leave an Unfulfilling Job

Sometimes, your job can wreak havoc on your soul. It's one thing to have to navigate work politics as a Black woman to ensure job security. It's another to have a job at a place that treats you like a workhorse, dehumanizes you, and makes you dread every day you have to work. Having an unfulfilling job does nothing more for you than pay your bills. And while sometimes, yes, that's the purpose of your job, at some point, having to go work at a place you hate to collect a paycheck is abusive. What is the purpose, sis? *What is the purpose?* Go find another place to work.

Leaving a job you hate requires strategy. First off, if you're in a position to quit without another job lined up, do it. Slide in your courtesy two weeks and peace out. However, if you can't just up and leave your job, make a plan. Decide what it is about your current job that you do not like. Make sure you seek the exact opposite. Search for jobs at different companies. Stay adjacent to the industry you're already in, or consider changing careers. Either way, you need to leave your awful work environment. You don't deserve to be treated with disrespect or disregard where you make money. It may feel like you do not have any other options, but the truth is, you do. You always have other choices. You just have to be brave enough to seek out other employment opportunities.

Join a Book Club

Warm your spirit up by gathering with other people who love books. A book club is a great way to make new friends and kiki with other women who enjoy reading. There are so many wonderful reasons for you to consider joining a book club. For instance, you'll expand on the types of genres you read by picking up books you might have otherwise ignored. In addition, you'll have a safe space to let out all your feelings about any particular book. Being in a book club will be one of the most rewarding self-care activities you try.

To find a book club to join, start at your local bookstore or library, inquiring about book clubs in your neighborhood. Or, you can begin your search online. Try websites like *Well-Read Black Girl*; this is a nationwide book club that allows you to join virtually or in-person at a bookstore near you. Plus, its goal is to amplify Black women writers (*hello!*). If you can't find an in-person book club, try a virtual meetup. And if that doesn't work for you, start your own. All you need is a couple friends and rotating book choices to get started.

Getting together with other book lovers helps you create relationships with people who make your soul happy. Reading is a great way for you to unwind and let go of any stress related to your daily encounters with microaggressions. Add a book club and you'll take your wellness to the next level.

Find Your Joy

Tapping into our Black Girl Joy is how we fight against a racist and sexist society trying to oppress us to death. As we find our joy, we will find our peace and path to radical self-care. Start by unlearning that you need to earn joy. Say to yourself every morning *I deserve joy*, until you believe it. Next, plan moments of happiness to look forward to—like, buying your favorite takeout every Friday. Follow up with creating a list of the things that make you smile and laugh. Do one of those activities at least once a week. Return to that list in times of distress. Lastly, explore different interests you have, finding one that makes you forget about your problems.

Trying to find joy as a Black woman in this world can be exhausting. You feel like you must earn it. In life, situations have happened that made us feel unworthy. For instance, when people disregard our words as we express our thoughts in a group setting. Or, when white people dismiss our feelings by telling us to *let it go* when we talk about intergenerational trauma created by things like the transatlantic slave trade or the war on drugs. And how about when people make us feel like outsiders by inquiring about our hair, skin, and body? It's damaging to the spirit. You don't need to prove to anyone or yourself that you are worthy of experiencing joy. You have a right to be happy and healthy. You just need to find *your* joy.

Write Down Your Ambitions

There is power in writing down your ambitions. Making your goals clear on paper lets your spirit and the world know exactly what you want to manifest in your life. Think of this as your written vision board. When you see and imagine the things you want to accomplish, you begin to believe you can achieve them. Penning your ambitions has its benefits, including increasing your spirit's direction, clarity, and motivation. You gain a deeper understanding of what you want as you read and reflect on what you have written. You also drown out the noise of society as it tries to discourage Black women. So, grab a notepad or your journal and start writing down your ambitions.

To practice this self-care activity, first reflect on the things that you want to accomplish and the way you want your life to look. Take out something to write on and make your list. One way to write down your ambitions is to create a list every year. And if you want extra focus, you can consider writing down your ambitions every month. It's a great way to evaluate your goals to change them as you see fit, and even cross off the ones you've achieved, as you stay focused on taking care of yourself. You won't worry about what others are doing because you'll be too busy hitting your own goals.

Connect with Black Women Online

Your day-to-day life can sometimes feel isolated. Connecting with Black women online can revive our spiritual connection to others and the world. You see, there's just something magical about Black women coming together. When we connect with other sistahs in the digital world, we feel heard, seen, supported, and valued. We tap into a conglomerate of Black women who just get us. Women who understand the trials, troubles, and triumphs we go through. In this circle, there's no proving our worth; it already exists. Simply put, gathering with other Black women is healing to your soul.

One way you can find an online crew is by joining a group on a social media site. For instance, *Facebook* allows users to create groups. Search for something that relates to your hobbies, like traveling or cooking. Look for a group that focuses on Black women who share your same interests. It's okay to search for things like "Black women travel group." You want to find a safe space for you to connect with other like-minded Black women.

As you build your tribe online, any feelings of loneliness will dissipate. It's important for you to have Black women you can connect with at the tips of your fingers and through your computer or phone screen. Your soul's wellness will improve, and you will be forever grateful for the connections you make as you carve out a space for your own connectivity and radical self-care.

Heal Your Mother Wound

As a woman, one of the strongest spiritual connections we have in this world is with our mother. The essence of who we are is mainly molded in our childhood by the kind of relationship we have with our primary caregiver, usually a mother. However, the fact is our mother passes on to us her mental, physical, and spiritual injuries. And if your mother was emotionally absent in your life, it creates a mother wound. And if your mother is also a Black woman, she has passed on to you her fears, pains, and internalized beliefs about her race and/or gender, beliefs that were formed because of her own experience with racial discrimination and gender prejudice. Have grace for your mama and heal your wound.

Begin this healing journey with self-reflection. Acknowledge your pain and give it a voice, such as journaling, writing an unsent letter to your mom, or going to therapy. There will also be some grieving for the childhood you wish you had. Next, create regular self-care practices that make you feel loved. You'll have to do some reparenting, treating yourself the way you wish your mother would've. Last, extend forgiveness and gratitude to your mother. She did the best she could with her own emotional and spiritual capacity. Be thankful that her faults led to your higher enlightenment of self. And remember, this is an ongoing practice for radical self-care. Remember that healing the wound caused by the relationship with your mother is essential to elevating your spiritual wellness.

Find a Fun Hobby

Get connected to yourself and lift your spirit by finding a hobby you can participate in for pure enjoyment. Our soul's wellness is at its best when we're having fun. Our spirit is free without any care or confinement. When we're feeling the pressures from society to behave or present ourselves in a certain way because we are a Black woman, engaging in a fun hobby allows our soul to let go and find joy.

To practice this self-care activity, first figure out what kind of hobby you want to do. This can be a sport, craft, etc. It's whatever you decide. Maybe you want to try a totally new activity. Or, perhaps you want to engage in something that reminds you of your childhood, like dodgeball. Make a decision and create a plan to begin your fun new hobby. Most importantly, continue to participate in your chosen activity as long as you are having fun for optimal self-care.

As you discover the enjoyment of your newfound hobby, you'll start to feel calmer. There might even be an extra pep in your step because your fun hobby allows you to have a total escape from society on your radical self-care journey. With you and your hobby, there's no one disrupting your peace with microaggressions or other racial slights. Just pure fun.

Explore Black Art

The beautiful thing about exploring Black art is that we get to witness the creative expression of Black people and get to know more about Black culture. It's empowering for our spirit to experience this. We reconnect to the stories of our culture from many members of the African diaspora. We build a bond to the new artistic creations Black people were moved to birth as a result of oppression. Black art has such a rich history for us to explore.

If you want to build a closer bond to Black art, start by exploring museums that showcase it. Here you will get a better understanding of the history and cultural influences of Black art. Next, find a Black artist you like and support them by purchasing their work. The deeper you go into your exploration of Black art, the closer your connection will become to Black culture.

Exploring Black art will fill you up with a sense of pride about your Black identity. It's inspiring to witness the work of Black artists because you get to see art that represents you.

Write a Letter to Yourself

Keep tabs on your growth by writing a letter to your future self. Your spiritual wellness is all about elevating your inner being. When we write a letter to our future self, we get to reflect on where we were and how far we have come. Creating space for you to examine your growth is imperative to your well-being. And as a person who constantly accomplishes great things, you need to stop, look back, and admire your life thus far. The best way to do this? Write a letter to yourself.

Start this self-care exercise by figuring out what future age you want to address your letter to. Begin writing. Include things about your current life. Express to your future self what you have been doing and some of your achievements. In addition, include something you hope to accomplish by the future age. After you're done writing your letter, put it in a place where you will not lose it. One suggestion: Tape it to the bottom of your desk. Most people don't get rid of their desks very often, so your letter will be around for a while, maybe even decades. Lastly, place a reminder in your phone's calendar to check for your letter at the future date.

In the long run, completing this fun self-care exercise will help you discover yourself. You'll have a sense of pride examining your past achievements and feelings of hope for what the future holds for you on your discovery of radical self-care. Start writing, sis.

Phone a Friend

Revive your soul by connecting with a friend on the phone. When we're feeling down, sometimes we just need to call up one of our girlies and have a good old-fashioned phone session. Talking on the phone helps you build stronger relationships and clearer communication skills. Phone calls are the perfect antidote for when we are unable to have a face-to-face hangout. They are also quite fun. Between swapping relationship stories, work mishaps, and life updates, laughter and validation are found in the midst of a phone conversation. And as a Black woman, coming together with a friend is what helps us heal. It's the best medicine. You'll feel whole as the person on the other side of the phone makes it evident that your existence is valued.

To complete this exercise most effectively, schedule a phone date with your friend. Create space to be on the phone at least two hours. Think of it like a regular meetup, but instead, you both get to do it from the comfort of your home. Ring up your girl and enjoy the phone conversation. Upgrade your phone session by talking via video chat if preferred. The more you talk, the better you'll feel. Radical self-care is a phone call away, so make plans to pick up your phone and call a friend. Your mood will improve, and your feelings of stress will decrease. There's a special type of healing that's reserved for Black women when we connect with each other. The collective sistah-hood pulls its strength from the ancestors and uplifts your spirit.

Ask for Help

Stop proudly calling yourself "the strong friend" and ask for help. While there's nothing wrong with being "the strong friend," you need to recognize that self-identifying as one is detrimental to your spirit. You're carrying burdens you don't need to hold on to by yourself. Sis, when's the last time you asked for support? Like, reached out to someone in a time of distress and willingly received the assistance that was provided?

Practice asking for help with people you trust who love you unconditionally. Start with folks you know and then work your way up to strangers. The more you ask for help, the easier it'll get. You'll humbly expect assistance that is fit for the queen you are.

And while you are certainly a queen, you've always got a nudge on your soul to uphold the "strong Black woman" trope. It's not your fault. Society literally beckons you to wear that trait with a badge of honor. You put on your strong Black woman cape when you tell folks "I'll figure it out." Or "I got this." There's nothing wrong with being a strong Black woman. But, obtaining assistance when you need it is also a sign of strength you will soon discover (or remember) on your radical self-care experience. Knowing when you've reached your limit and need help is a special kind of superpower. It's releasing all feelings of anxiety in your soul and allowing yourself to trust others to do their part for your benefit. You can do it.

Go Volunteer

Create a stronger connection to your community by volunteering. Donating our time to an organization will improve our spiritual wellness. When we help other people, we tend to feel better. So in times where you might feel helpless and like no one cares about your existence because you are Black, shock your system by volunteering and caring for others. You will see value and purpose in those whom you help.

To complete this exercise, first think about the kind of place you would like to volunteer. Next, research the available organizations in your community. After you locate some places where you'd like to volunteer, reach out to those organizations. Coordinate with your schedule and go. Consider incorporating being a volunteer into your self-care routine at least once a month. If possible, upgrade your volunteer time to once a week for a more radical self-care experience. The more you volunteer, the more you'll realize there is more to life than your day-to-day activities. As you continue to serve, your worldview will expand—and so will the well-being of your soul. Volunteering is truly the gift that keeps on giving. Give back and find wellness.

Learn a New Language

Learn a new language to deepen your connection to the world. There are so many languages spoken all over the globe. Learning a language that is different from the language(s) we use can be an exciting experience. By attempting to learn a new language, we open up our spirit and mind to different cultures. We get to see how people live, talk, eat, etc. We also get to challenge ourselves with something new. Learning a new language also allows us to tap into our African ancestral roots because our ancestors all spoke different languages.

To learn a new language, first decide which one you want to dive into. Once you decide, look up classes for your chosen language at your local community college or further education school. Most of these schools have language classes that you can take for a low price. Additionally, you can also search online via a language learning center or website and connect with a language teacher. However you decide to learn a new language, go at your own pace, and enjoy the learning process.

All in all, learning a new language is a fun self-care activity. You'll learn a lot about yourself. It forces you to move beyond your comfort zone in a healthy way for radical self-care. And as you learn the language of your choice, you will begin to inhabit the culture of the language and expand the vibe of your spirit.

Read a Spiritual Book

One great way to build a better connection to your inner being is to read a spiritual book. Reading these kinds of books has many benefits. First off, reading encourages us to learn. When we read a spiritual book, we increase our knowledge about life and self while welcoming a positive change into our atmosphere. Additionally, picking up a spiritual book will help us feel closer to our ancestors. Spirituality was and is an integral part of Black culture. From African deities to Christian faiths, Black people love some spirituality. It's how our ancestors survived such brutal treatment during the times of colonization. That being said, spiritual books aren't just about religions. They also include themes related to connecting deeper to the world and others, thinking outside your immediate perspective. Head to the spirituality section wherever you buy books and check it out for yourself.

To find the right spiritual book to indulge in, pick one that sparks your interest. Or, you can do some much-needed reflection and pick up a book that meets any of your spiritual needs. Be sure to read at your own pace, as books in this particular genre often require some heavy emotional and spiritual cleansing.

Spiritual books help us build up confidence and improve our mood. We also learn more about different ways to build up our spiritual wellness. After you're done reading, you will feel motivated to continue to work toward your higher self on your road to discovering radical self-care.

Practice Radical Honesty with Yourself

Okay, it's time to get real, real quick. To achieve the benefits of radical self-care, we must practice being brutally honest with ourselves. This means looking within and examining where we are getting in the way of our wellness. You see, sis, we are used to putting the needs of our mental, physical, and spiritual health aside. It's not our fault. Society has conditioned us to think that our needs are less important than others. We have been trained to lie to ourselves about what we really require to thrive. Time to toss this thinking aside. Get really freaking honest with yourself, so you can live your best darn life.

To begin practicing radical honesty with yourself, you must increase your self-awareness. Start looking at every area of your life with a rational lens. Get real with yourself about your thoughts and actions, resisting the need to justify any self-sabotaging behavior you engage in. Face your reality. Next, examine when negative emotions like jealousy or anger arise in you toward people and situations. Don't judge yourself for these emotions, but simply ask yourself, *Why am I feeling this way?* The more you pause to explore what's going on within, the better you will get at being radically honest with yourself.

As you pursue being very honest *with you*, you will eventually also become very honest with others on your self-care journey. Feelings of shame will dissipate because you'll learn to have compassion for yourself and feel confident to move forward toward your highest self.

Practice Being Nonjudgmental

When it comes to elevating your spiritual wellness, being judgmental of self and others can get in the way. It's important to note that there is a difference between making judgments and being judgmental. Our mind naturally makes judgments, filtering out what we perceive as good, bad, and neutral. Being judgmental is a defense mechanism, something we might've picked up from constantly having to alter the way we present our racial identity in order to be accepted by others as Black women. It blocks our ability to boldly pursue total wellness. When we're being judgmental, we're jumping to conclusions without obtaining all the facts. And sometimes, we're not even aware that we're being judgmental. So, it's time to practice being nonjudgmental.

First off, you must understand what being nonjudgmental means. When you are being nonjudgmental, you are making a conscious effort to not act emotionally or spiritually on every new piece of information you're given. To do this, you must be willing to be self-aware. Anytime a judgmental thought pops up into your mind, instantly push it away or examine it. Ask yourself why you're being judgmental. This is an ongoing practice that you can pursue by being mindful of the energy you receive and emit on your path to radical self-care.

As you practice being nonjudgmental, you will find inner peace. Your spirit will feel lighter and clearer. Just be sure to not be judgmental of yourself as you attempt to practice being nonjudgmental.

Become a Mentor

Connect to the younger generation by becoming a mentor. Being a mentor requires us to activate our spiritual wellness frequently. We must be self-aware, which means knowing our inner being very well. Additionally, we must be great at creating bonds with individuals who will supersede our existence. When we become a mentor, we help pay it forward to the next generation by offering tools for them to succeed.

There are many ways you can become a mentor. It can be through your industry, your school, or your local community organization. Most people become mentors by being approached. Honestly, this is the best way to do it. You want to mentor someone who wants to be a mentee. Aim to mentor fellow Black women or girls. Doing this will give you the satisfaction of giving back to others whose paths are similar to yours.

Ultimately, becoming a mentor is all about motivating and encouraging others. As you mentor another Black woman, you will be providing more power to the collective sistah-hood. Your guidance and advice will create a ripple effect for generations to come.

Check In with Your Spirit

Take care of your well-being by checking in on the condition of your soul. The most important part about taking care of our spirit is making sure it is well balanced and at ease. You will know your soul is irked when you do not have inner peace. Some signs that your spirit is experiencing imbalance are negative emotions, including feelings of guilt, shame, sadness, anger, or anxiety. Listen to your gut when these emotions arise. As a Black woman, we've been taught by society to ignore these negative feelings, that we can suppress them and keep on going. Well, sis. You can do that, but it'll only result in spiritual illness. Hence, the need to have regular check-ins with your spirit.

Oftentimes, you may not know something has impacted your soul until it shows up as unexpected anger or sadness. To prevent misguided emotions, perform a wellness check on your spirit weekly. This can look like having some form of quiet time to scan your inner being for anything that is disrupting you from vibrating higher. And when you notice something is off, make a note and then act. Tap into one of your self-care activities for your soul and give yourself a grace period to return to your original self and resume your radical self-care.

Spiritual check-ins are essential to maintaining our overall wellness. The more we evaluate our soul, the more we build self-awareness. Being aware of self will help you and your spirit soar to new heights of well-being.

Learn to Forgive Yourself

Accept a new way of being by learning to forgive yourself. By nature, we are wired to be hard on ourselves. It's easier to beat yourself up than it is to be kind. We don't really get second chances as a Black woman, so we try to leave little room for error with all we do. This leads to us being unable to forgive ourselves when we make human mistakes. What good is it to our soul if we're constantly operating from a space of unforgiveness of self? Nothing. Nada. Zilch. That's why you must learn to forgive yourself.

To begin the work of self-forgiveness, you must first acknowledge your mistakes. Then, think of each wrongdoing as a learning experience. Follow up by having a conversation with that supercritical inner voice of yours. Talk back to it by journaling your feelings or telling it out loud that you will not listen to what it has to say. Sometimes, self-talk can really get your spirit going in the right direction. Most importantly, have grace for yourself as you work through learning to forgive yourself on your radical self-care discovery.

The journey of self-forgiveness is an ongoing one. However, the more you practice, the more you will instinctively be forgiving of yourself. The result of this exercise is that you will maintain a peaceful and joyful spirit.

Let Go of Your Personal Timeline

Do you have a personal timeline? You know, married by twenty-five, kids by thirty, house by thirty-two, etc. Sometimes, society makes us feel like we are behind because our milestones don't match with those of the average human. The question is: Who said you were meant to be average? You're a dynamic Black woman. Nothing about you is average. Remember that. And because you are unique, you have every right to operate your life however you see fit. Therefore, tying yourself to a milestone timeline you made up in your head is only causing your soul to feel troubled. Let your personal timeline go.

To do that, you just have to accept the reality of your life. There's nothing wrong with the way it is going. This doesn't mean you shouldn't have hopes and dreams about reaching certain goals by a certain time, but don't let not hitting those milestones at that time make you feel like a failure. Whose timeline are you on? Yours or your Higher Power's? When your soul is in alignment with the ways of your spiritual divine, incredible things happen. And if nothing you desire has happened yet, then it is not your time for that particular milestone. Continue to live your life and make radical self-care changes.

As you work on letting go of your personal timeline, you will begin to feel less anxious. You will have inner peace. This practice will lead you to your higher self, teaching you to trust your spiritual beliefs.

Correct Your Name's Mispronunciation

Make sure others put some respect on your name. When someone mispronounces our name and refuses to try to say it correctly because they "can't say it," this is a microaggression. Because we are Black, they don't feel like our name is worth trying to pronounce. And, you appeasing their inability to even try to say your name right is a trauma response. You don't want to cause trouble. Well, it's time to shake the table. For too long, Black people have been discriminated against, turned down for jobs, and ridiculed because our names sound "too Black." Take back your name by unabashedly asking people to pronounce it correctly.

To do this, you must first release any feelings of shame you have around your name. Your name was given to you by your parents, so it most definitely has a special meaning. Honor that. And if you want to beat the awkwardness around the way someone tries to pronounce your name, come up with phonetic tips that can help them say it the right way. Asking others to say your name correctly is literally your birthright. Literally.

So, going forward, as you meet new people, practice this exercise on your journey to radical self-care. The more times you do it, the more you will grow comfortable with asking people to say your name correctly. This will help keep your spirit at peace because you are honoring the essence of who you are.

Choose to Let Love In

Sometimes, it's hard to let love enter our spirit as a Black woman. We already don't trust a lot of people because we always have to have our guard up to protect our well-being. And when that wall is up, it can be hard to knock it down. Especially if we've experienced betrayal in friendships, romantic relationships, or family dynamics. However, allowing ourselves to be vulnerable and accept love is beneficial to the wellness of our soul.

To let love in, we must first examine why we have a hard time accepting love. Take some time to yourself to really reflect and explore the early messages you received about love within your family. Was love conditional? Did you have to do something to earn it? Think about it. Once you're ready to let love in, you must practice being vulnerable with safe people. Start with opening up to friends and other loved ones you trust. Share something you have never told them. It's important to choose safe people to be vulnerable with because the right people will react in a supportive and loving way. This will teach you that it's okay to accept love as you continue to develop on your radical self-care experience.

Choosing to let love in is a practice you'll have to work through almost every day. When we allow love into our lives, the barriers on our soul break away. Love is the key to life. The more love you have, the happier you'll be. Go be vulnerable, sis.

Stop Ranting on Social Media

Listen, social media is great. You can make connections with people, have some good laughs, and get informed about anything and everything all at once. Not to mention, the Black communities that have formed on most apps are top-tier. However, using social media as your personal diary is not good for your spirit. Social media is a very public place, and sometimes we might forget that as we use our fingers to post a rant about something that frustrates us. Our thoughts matter, but the fact is that when we rant on social media, we are seeking some form of validation. And if we don't get it immediately, our mood can go from bad to worse. In addition, posting to social media nonstop while scrolling endlessly is opening ourselves up to receiving all kinds of energy we may not want in our spirit.

Stop ranting on social media and express yourself in a healthier way. If you're feeling angry and you want to rant about something, consider one of these alternatives: calling or texting a friend, writing in your journal, or going for a walk until you calm down. Choosing to put down your phone and vent in a way that won't leave you exposed online is spiritual growth and radical self-care. Try it the next time you feel like using your Twitter fingers.

Sing Your Favorite Song

Set your spirit free by singing along to your favorite song. This activity will reconnect you to ancestors, such as enslaved members of the African diaspora who sang religious folk songs called spirituals to express their faith, as well as their sorrows. In addition, music has always been a central part of Black culture worldwide. So when we sing, we connect to the collective Black community who have used music as a way to express themselves through the pressures of oppression. Wuddup, hip-hop. What's good, grime. When their voices about injustices wouldn't be heard, they said it through the music. So, turn on your favorite song and do as your ancestors would do: Sing.

This activity can be done whenever and wherever you have privacy and the ability to sing as loud as you want. A suggested place to sing: the shower. To complete this exercise, simply turn on your song of choice (*cough* *anything with Beyoncé* *cough*) and let your vocal cords go. Don't worry about being in tune. Just enjoy your song without a care in the world.

After you're done singing, your soul will feel at peace. Singing helped alleviate whatever burdens you were carrying from your stress and anxiety. Hit a note and let it carry you further down the road to more radical self-care.

Light a Scented Candle

Give your senses a luxury treat with a scented candle. After a long day of work from having to deal with your well-meaning white coworkers, lighting a candle and relaxing is exactly what you need. Invigorating our senses with the smell of a candle is healing to our soul. The benefits of burning a candle include improving our mood, calming our mind, and creating a relaxing ambiance. Grab your favorite scented candle and enjoy a relaxing evening.

For a quick calming fix, take your favorite scented candle and light it up. Make sure it is not near anything flammable. Dim your lights and do a relaxing activity, such as reading, stretching, or listening to music. For a more elongated self-care activity, draw yourself a bubble bath, light your candle, and place it on the side of the tub. Next, turn down your bathroom lights, grab your book, and get in the water. Enjoy your relaxing evening as you soak and read for a bit. And if none of these activities spark your interest, enjoy your candle whichever way works best for you.

After relaxing with a lighted candle, your mood will be lifted. You will be calm, and possibly sleepy. If you have time, settle down for a nap and enjoy additional benefits of radical self-care.

Play with a Puppy

Manage your overall wellness by playing with a dog. According to the Centers for Disease Control and Prevention (CDC), the benefits of having a pet (like a puppy) include managing our feelings of loneliness and depression, as well as decreasing our blood pressure and cholesterol levels, which is highly significant for Black women. Thus, we need to find a dog to play with as soon as possible to improve our overall wellness.

There's just something special about dogs, especially puppies. These animals are usually very playful, and it's beneficial for our spirit to be around such boisterous energy. The free spirit of the dog can rub off on us and help us calm down when stressed. We'll also feel more open and free-spirited.

If you already have a dog, plan to have some extra time with your pup in the name of self-care. But if you don't own a dog, nor have a friend who will let you watch their puppy, consider volunteering at an animal shelter. You'll get to interact with all kinds of dogs and improve your wellness in the process as you continue your radical self-care.

Acknowledgments

When I was approached to write this book, it felt like the stars aligned and God called me for this assignment. Empowering Black women is at the core of my life's passion and purpose. Thank you to my editor at Adams Media, Leah D'Sa, for recognizing my capabilities to complete this project. Thank you to my developmental editor, Shaundale Rénā. I am so glad that our paths as Black women crossed and we were able to collaborate on this divine assignment. Thank you to Tess Armstrong, whose illustrations brought every page to life. And to everyone at Adams Media and Simon & Schuster who assisted in publishing this work, thank you. Thank you for handling this book's subject matter delicately. Furthermore, I want to acknowledge those who impacted my life and the creation of this book.

Foremost, I am grateful to my family who has allowed me to forge a path of my own. To my mother, Victoria Adeeyo, who passed onto another life too soon and taught me the power of forgiveness and faith. Her sweet spirit is greatly missed. I am thankful for my father, Kola Adeeyo, for his many sacrifices that ensured my ability to pursue my dreams. His unconditional love is the cause of my unwavering self-confidence.

I am beyond blessed to have many sister-friends whose steadfast support got me through the hardest times in my life. Thank you to Fope Adesina, Miriam Agwai, Damilola Akinola, Allycia Atania, Maritess Balmater, Rasheda Crockett, Tiffany Peng Hwa,

Kara Murphy, Deborah Ni, Victoria Okusanya, Sabine Paul, and Rhapsodi Pierre-Jacques. Without your grace, love, and encouragement, I wouldn't have been able to stand in my truth, change careers, and achieve personal growth.

Thank you to my professional mentors. Susan Schulz, my first boss at *Cosmopolitan,* who saw my value in the workplace when others didn't and helped me go from journalism to social work. Lynne Burroughs and Thandiwe Gregory, my clinical supervisors, who provided me with insight and guidance as I grew into my role as a psychiatric social worker.

I also can't forget to thank the queen, Beyoncé, whose music pushed me through the stressful moments of writing this book. Her artistry inspires me every day, as well as her commitment to changing the world, which gives me courage to do the same.

Most importantly, I am thankful for Black women. Each one of you is the reason I leaped at the opportunity to write this book. I see you. I am committed to elevating our wellness.

Finally, thank you to my longtime hairdresser, Ron Lewis, who once told me, "Your pen is your sword. Use it." I am and I will.

Index

About the Author

Oludara Adeeyo is a psychotherapist based in Los Angeles. She works as a psychiatric social worker, where she assists individuals experiencing homelessness, as well as severe and persistent mental illnesses. Oludara is passionate about helping people improve their overall well-being, especially Black women. Before becoming a clinical social worker, Oludara spent seven-plus years working as a writer and editor. She has been an associate web editor at *Cosmopolitan* and the managing editor at *XXL*. Oludara grew up in Edison, New Jersey. She loves Beyoncé, hot yoga, cooking, and watching telenovelas.